Primarily Patchwork

The Quilt Enthusiast Shop
1439 Buffalo Road
Rochester, New York 14624
(716) 235-4670
TUES.–SAT. 10–5

Patchwork Pillow Utilizing Basic Techniques 3

Distinctive patchwork through the use of fabric selection, combining prints, working with color. Getting down to the essentials: Template making, hand piecing, designing, recording designs. The whys of quilting, preparing for quilting. Fancy pillow edgings for a distinct look. Professional stuffing hints.

Hexagons and Other Hand Pieced Patterns 25

Choose from our large selection of pattern sizes and arrangements of hexagons. Color plates and illustrations give a glimpse at the hexagon's potential. Fifteen all-time favorite blocks with their full-size pattern pieces and color plates give you further experience with hand piecing.

Machine Patchwork 53

Achieving accuracy with or without a template. Assembly line approach to joining pattern pieces. Ten suggested patterns to utilize machine techniques. Detailed discussions on Log Cabin and Hexagon Beauty -- how to adapt them for projects.

Eight Piece Centers 70

Immediate success can be achieved with these step-by-step illustrated instructions for sewing patterns with eight piece centers. Eight blocks with suggested design variations are given.

Curved Seam Work 83

Understanding the elements of marking and pinning can give a novice perfect results. Twelve arrangements of Drunkard's Path are given along with four other curved seam patterns.

Clamshell 90

Stunning arrangements of clamshells are shown in color plates and black and white illustrations inspiring projects for wearables and usables.

Alphabetical Index of Patterns (with sizes)

List of Patterns by Size

Patchwork Pillow Utilizing Basic Techniques

THE FIRST PROJECT - A PATCHWORK, QUILTED PILLOW WITH RUFFLE

The patchwork, quilted pillow is a must, and should be fully understood and then carefully executed. It will provide challenge in designing and selecting printed fabrics while teaching the basic hand piecing methods. If your imagination and enthusiasm carry you away while designing this, you can always expand the design or change the project into a small wall hanging, baby quilt or lap throw.

BASIC SUPPLIES NEEDED

Read over this supply list, and you'll be surprised to find that you already have most of the items needed.

    One sheet stiff sandpaper (medium grit)
    Lead pencil
    Dressmaker's pencil
    Dressmaker's beeswax
    Dressmaker's carbon paper
    Dressmaker's pins
    Pencil sharpener
    Rubber cement
    Six-inch clear (or see through) ruler
    Twelve-inch clear ruler
    Small roll of masking tape
    Sharp dressmaker's scissors
    Paper cutting scissors
    Notebook paper
    Graph paper, four grids to the inch
    Four fabrics, ¼ yd. each for pillow front & back
    Fabric for ruffle, approximately ¾ yd.
    Polyester sheet batting, firmly bonded
    Loose polyester fiberfill, 1 lb.
    Needles, betweens or sharps, sizes 5/10
    Thread, polyester core, cotton wrapped to match
        fabric
    Old sheet or muslin for backing fabric (approxi-
        mately ½ yd.)
    Quilting thread to correspond with fabric.

CHOOSING YOUR FABRIC FOR PATCHWORK

Fabrics for your first few projects in patchwork should be made of cotton or cotton/polyester. The higher the cotton fiber content, the better "hand" or feel the fabric will have. Choose a fabric that is firmly woven but soft and pliable, not stiff or ridged. Look for a fabric that looks and feels similar to the fabrics used in your sheets or pillowcases. A light-weight but firmly woven fabric will make it easier for cutting patches with sharp long corners. A soft fabric will be easier to quilt through than a hard or heavily sized fabric. Check the label on the bolt to see that the fabric is colorfast and preshrunk. Try to buy the best quality you can afford for your handwork. Some of the wash and wear fabrics are excellent, and don't overlook the broadcloths or percales.

For your first experiences with patchwork, avoid woolens, corduroy, felt, silk fabrics, heavy denim or canvas. Also avoid knit fabrics for the time being. Stay away from fabrics that are thin or transparent such as voile, dotted swiss or organza. Patches cut from these fabrics will have to be underlined, so they are not recommended for a beginning patchwork student. Fabrics with a printed patchwork pattern are also not recommended.

GOOD SOURCES OF FABRICS

Suitable fabric for patchwork can come from many sources. I suggest to beginning students that they check their remnants at home, then check with their neighbors, especially the mothers in the neighborhood who sew for little girls, or the grandmother down the block who is always making clothes for grandchildren. You will find that their castoffs, or remnants from sewing projects, tend to be very suitable for patchwork. After you have scoured the neighborhood, visit your local stores that specialize in selling remnants and bolt ends. These stores often carry the same fabrics as the larger department stores, but they sell bolt ends or the last three or four yards from bolts of fabrics used by garment manufacturers. These will usually be free of flaws and reasonably priced.

Let your local fabric stores know you are interested in patchwork. The owner of the store will in turn purchase fabrics of interest to her immediate community and may tend to start stocking more woven, small printed cottons in the future, and start lowering her inventory of polyester knits. If certain colors or prints are of interest to you, let her know She will usually be happy to keep her eyes open for what you want when she is selecting her new bolts for the coming season.

Most stores that sell fabrics have a remnant counter or bin that can yield a real treasure if you dig deep enough. This can also turn out to be the opposite case, and you may end up with a "great find" that is really a poor purchase because of a large hole or a flaw that runs through the entire piece.

Combining Your Fabrics

Nothing is more stimulating to good patchwork than using a wide variety of fabrics. To do this well takes study and practice and then more study and practice. We encourage students to think in terms of prints and color when combining fabrics.

HINTS ON PRINTS

Select fabrics with small prints. When you see a print fabric, remember that when it is used in patchwork, you will see only a small piece or patch of the fabric. To test a fabric to see if it is suitable for the triangle pillow project, cut a 3½ inch triangle from the middle of a sheet of notebook paper and place the sheet of paper on the bolt of fabric. The print that shows is the amount of print you will see in your patch. If you are looking at a bolt of fabric with a large print, you would only get some of the print in your patch. Generally, you want all patches cut from one fabric to show the same print.

Try to combine fabrics with different scales of print. Having a variety of size or scale will give your patchwork richness.

Vary the figure within the prints. Choosing prints with all one motif, such as flowers, will be a little boring. Try for a dot or seashell, curving lines or waves for a more interesting effect.

Poor combination.

Good combination of scale and motif.

COLOR REVIEW

Color selection is probably the most important part of designing patchwork. Review the basic colors and their relationships.

The primary colors are red, yellow and blue, and from them all other colors are made. The secondary colors, orange, green and purple, are made by combining the primary colors. For example, blue and yellow mixed make green. Color Wheel I shows the primary and secondary colors. Tertiary colors are formed when secondary colors are combined, and are shown in Color Wheel II.

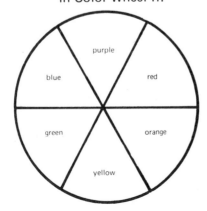

Primary and secondary colors.

How to Work With Color

Color families

The following rules can be easily applied to fabrics for any patchwork project. You will find that color selection for patchwork differs from working with color for wearing apparel. After teaching hundreds of students the basics of patchwork, we have developed these three rules to simplify color selection.

RULE 1: <u>Choose fabrics from one color family</u>. This means choosing various prints and/or solid colors, but all from one color family. The range of color within a color family is very large because of color value and tertiary colors, as pointed out in Color Wheel III. No matter what you wish to combine, all fabrics from one color family will work well together.

RULE 2: <u>Choose fabrics from two different color families.</u> The color families could be contrasting or on opposite sides of the color wheel, such as blue and orange, or red and green. <u>Analogous</u> colors would be two color families lying next to each other on the color wheel. Combining fabrics from the orange and yellow color family is a good example of using complementary colors. Remember to select fabrics from the whole range of yellow and orange. This means using as many varied shades of oranges or yellows as possible. Mix deep orange, red-orange, dull beige-orange, orange prints on cream or white and so on.

RULE 3: <u>Choose fabrics from different color families, but all having the same value or intensity.</u> For example, use all bright colors, ruby red, sky blue, bold yellow, grass green; or you could combine a variety of colors using all pastels or soft colors, such as light pink, soft blue, pale green, etc. A variety of colors, whether solids or solids and prints, will work well together as long as their color intensities are the same.

A <u>color family</u> would consist of a primary or secondary color and its surrounding tertiary colors. For example, the red color family would consist of red, purple-red, and orange-red.

<u>Value</u> has also been introduced to Color Wheel III. Now when we speak of the red color family we mean the following: dark red, red, light red, light purple-red, dark purple-red, light orange-red and dark orange-red.

If a printed fabric has a white or cream background, assign it to a color family according to the dominating color in that print. For instance, a cream fabric with a splash of red roses, green stems, a small amount of yellow and orange within the roses, would probably be labeled as belonging to the red family because of the dominating roses. A white fabric with blue rocking horses, each adorned with purple plumes, black hooves and green saddles, would be classified as belonging to the blue color family since this is the most abundant color used in the print.

Plan your patchwork projects with your own color preferences. Choose colors that you really enjoy, colors that make you feel and look good, or colors that will enhance the setting your patchwork is placed in.

Colors tend to evoke certain moods or feelings. Soft colors will give the feeling of age or antiqueness. Bright colors or patterns stand out more vividly and are stunning in modern settings. Study the color plates in this book to get more ideas of how color can be used in different settings to enhance the mood you are trying to create.

Preparing Fabrics for Patchwork

Make it a habit to throw all the fabrics you want to use for patchwork right into the washer and dryer, in most cases as soon as you get them home. Separate the fabrics according to darks and lights and use very hot water. The hot soapy water will help soften the new stiff fabric and remove the excess sizing. This is also a good way to be sure the fabric is pre-shrunk, colorfast and fairly wrinkle free. When the fabrics come out of the dryer, look them over for any that have excess wrinkles. These should be set aside and not used for patchwork.

If someone gives you a lot of scraps of cotton and you don't feel they have previously been machine washed, don't just throw them into the washer. Their many cut edges will fray and ravel with the washing machine's agitation and the scraps can become tangled and matted. To eliminate this problem, use a nylon net or laundering bag. The net will allow the water to flow through and around the pieces, but it keeps the scraps together. There will be little or no tangling. Most fabric stores sell this type of laundering bag. Check your mail order catalog if you can't find them elsewhere.

All fabrics should be ironed and folded before being stored, or before they are marked and cut for patchwork. Try folding fabrics with the print side showing instead of turning the prints to the inside like the clerks in the store so often do. It will be easier to look through a stack of fabrics if their printed side is showing. If you want a fabric for its wrong side, then that should be the side showing when placed in a stack.

One student keeps her small scraps of fabric in see-through plastic food storage bags. This way they don't become lost in her large pile of fabrics, never to be seen again. They are easy to spot through the clear plastic.

PATCHWORK — BY HAND OR MACHINE

Many of the traditional patchwork patterns would be exceedingly difficult if not impossible to do by machine, so we purposely encourage beginning patchwork students to first learn hand sewing techniques. You would be limiting yourself to a very narrow range of pattern selection if you could not do hand piecing. Granted, many patterns can be done with a sewing machine and on Page 53 we give you detailed information and patterns for machine work. However, for the first project, making a pillow with the triangle shape, plan to do it by hand. After finishing this project, when you select any traditional pattern in the future, you can draw upon your skill and knowledge and decide when and where you want to use machine or hand sewing.

Making a Template

MAKING A TEMPLATE (PATTERN)

The first project, a patchwork pillow, uses one shape, a triangle. Place a sheet of graph paper over the triangle pattern given below and using a ruler to guide your pencil, trace the pattern as accurately as possible. Be sure to also trace the grain line within the triangle. Next, after applying a good coat of rubber cement to the back side of your tracing, press the graph paper down to the paper side or smooth side of a sheet of stiff sandpaper. Smooth out any wrinkles and wait a few minutes for the rubber cement to dry.

Use old scissors to cut the triangle pattern from the sandpaper. Be very accurate and cut smoothly, because your pattern will never be more accurate than it is now. You can test your pattern or template for accuracy by tracing around it with a pencil onto a new sheet of graph paper. Giving the template a 180 turn, line the diagonal edges even with each other and trace around the two remaining sides. You should have a perfect 3½ inch square with a diagonal line cutting through it. Adjust your pattern if necessary.

Stiff sandpaper or sandpaper with a sheet of acetate or plastic film cemented to its paper side is suggested for all template making, because it gives you a firm edge to trace around. It also grips the fabric, preventing it from moving as you trace around the edges of the template.

If your fabric is holding firm to the pattern, but shifting around on your work surface, tape a large sheet of sandpaper with the grit side up to your table top. This should hold the fabric firmly.

Excellent plastic or metal templates can be purchased in a wide range of sizes and shapes. These templates do not wear or soften at the corners and they always remain accurate no matter how many times you trace around them. Their surface has been roughed on one side, so when they are placed on fabric, they tend to grip the cloth.

For the pillow project plan to cut eight patches from each of your four different fabrics for a total of thirty-two patches or triangles. For all patchwork designs you want to sew by hand, the techniques on pages 8, 12, & 14, should be followed.

Grain line

Grain line

Tracing the Template Onto Fabric

Always draw onto the wrong side of the fabric. To do this, smooth your fabric out over a firm surface or table top with the wrong side of the fabric facing up. Many fabrics have no wrong side, such as ginghams and solid colors. Look at your fabric, and if both sides look the same, you can decide it has no wrong side. However, if one side looks lighter or washed out, that is the wrong side.

Trim off the tightly woven selvage edge of the fabric. If your fabric does shrink, even slightly, the selvage with its high thread count will shrink more than the rest of the fabric. This can cause puckering within your patches, so trim away this potential problem.

Place the template on the wrong side of the fabric, matching its grain line with the lengthwise or crosswise grain of the fabric. Using a sharp lead pencil, trace around the template. This will be your seam or sewing line. If your fabric is dark and the pencil mark doesn't show, use a dressmaker's pencil which is available at fabric stores in pale blue, pink or white. Unlike dressmaker's chalk, a dressmaker's pencil can be sharpened in a pencil sharpener and it is easy to handle. Keep a small hand pencil sharpener available in your patchwork supplies because a dull pencil point will leave a very broad mark which sometimes appears as a dirt streak from the right side of the fabric.

Add a ¼ inch seam allowance to each patch. This can be done quickly and easily using a clear plastic ruler. Students find the short 6 inch ruler easiest to handle. Place a strip of masking tape on the top surface of the ruler, leaving ¼ inch exposed along the ruler's length.

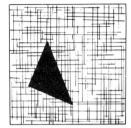

Incorrect placement of template

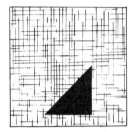

Template placed with the grain of the fabric

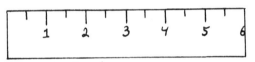

Clear plastic ruler

Masking tape placed on top surface of ruler.

TRACING THE TEMPLATE ONTO FABRIC

Lay the ruler down on the fabric with the edge of the masking tape even with the traced pencil line. Note the ruler is extending ¼ inch beyond. Trace along the edge of the ruler and you have added a ¼ inch seam allowance. Do this to every side or edge of each patch or shape. This second pencil line will be your cutting line.

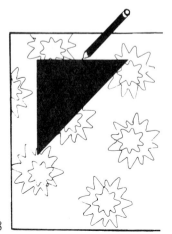 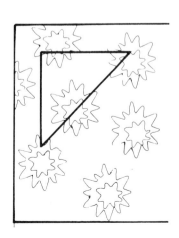 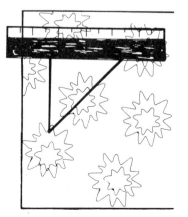 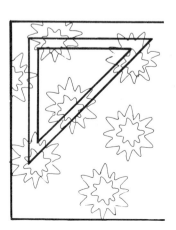

Record Your Designs

CUTTING THE FABRIC PATCHES

Use very sharp dressmaker's scissors to get patches with smooth, jag-free edges. Fabric shears can be taken to most yardage stores to be resharpened, if necessary. The cost is low and the improved cutting edge is worth the time you may have to give up while your shears are being sharpened.

RECORD DESIGNS

When you come upon a design that has an impact on you, record it so you will be able to reconstruct it after you have tried more approaches. After you get the feel of it, it only takes a few minutes to record a design, and it will give you greater breadth in good design selection.

Use a sheet of graph paper, four grids to the inch, sometimes referred to as ¼ inch graph paper, to record each fabric and its placement. Give each fabric a number for quick recording as shown below. With practice you will also be able to visualize the fabric you will want for the ruffle. If you can visualize using bands in your design, record their suggested placement.

1 = Brown
2 = Pink Print
3 = Brown Check
4 = Brown & Pink Print

BE A DESIGNER - SOME BASIC APPROACHES

Designing can be fun, if you let it. Some students have a hard time trying to experiment with their patches, while others get carried away and find many good designs to choose from. If design ideas are slow in taking shape with your fabrics, try each of the following four design approaches. These will help you get the feel of designing and manipulating your patches while still keeping a balanced design. We encourage students to try these approaches one at a time, using all thirty-two patches on each layout. When you find a layout or design that looks good with your fabrics, record it as described.

If you are trying some of the pillow tops shown in Color Plates 1 through 26, you may find that a particular design done with your fabrics gives a totally different effect. It may even appear disappointing. This is because some fabrics, such as pastels, or fabrics with soft, quaint, over-all prints, will appear at their best in clustered arrangements. The same fabrics set in another arrangement may appear lost, even confused. The same can be said for bold, strong colors and prints. They may not appear at their best, design-wise, when done in an arrangement in which soft colors look smashing. It is important to experiment with your fabric selection, and see what they suggest to you in the way of a good design.

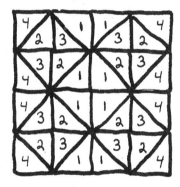

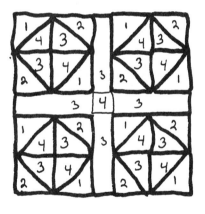

To speed up marking and eliminate wasting fabric, draw a second seam allowance on the long diagonal edge. Place your template against this second line and trace around the two remaining sides. Add seam allowances to the two remaining sides. With sharp scissors, cut the two triangle patches apart on their common cutting line.

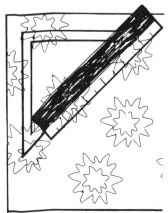
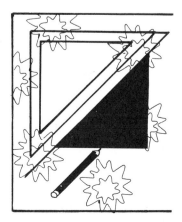
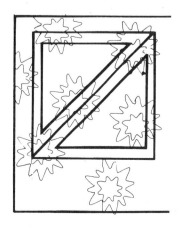

Designing Techniques

DESIGN APPROACH 1 — HORIZONTAL OR DIAGONAL MOVEMENT

Select from your four fabrics the one or two that are strongest in color or the ones that tend to catch your eye; that jump out at you. Arrange these in a horizontal or diagonal formation and then fill in around them with the rest of your fabrics. This design formation will tend to carry your eye across the design from side to side or from corner to corner.

To get a good horizontal or diagonal movement, you may need to cut more patches of your strongest color or colors. Be sure that you still use some of all four different fabrics to maintain a rich, varied finished product.

Keep your design balanced. The sketch shows both a balanced and unbalanced design. Your eye will not be allowed to flow across an unbalanced arrangement. Try squinting to quickly identify whether a design is balanced or not.

An interesting variation can be done with the horizontal design approach. Try reversing its order, starting from the center and working outward. Many variations can result from this easy design method.

Bands can add to the richness of your total design as you will see in Color Plate 1. Bands were also added to the top and bottom edges of the pillow top in Color Plate 2. Always experiment. Take a good design and experiment with it further. You will never know whether or not bands would add to your design unless you try them.

DESIGN APPROACH 2 - FOUR TIME REPEAT

Using eight triangles, two of each color, make a small arrangement. It may not look stunning at this point. Next, repeat this small arrangement or unit three more times and a nicely balanced design will appear. There are numerous ways to start your basic unit of eight, so try this design approach several times, each time rearranging your basic unit of eight and then repeating it three more times.

It is important when doing this design variation to use all thirty-two of your fabric triangles. Take care not to judge your design too early. Don't have just two units composed in front of you and decide that a good design is not developing. Use all thirty-two of your patches and then judge the total design.

The four-time repeat lends itself very well to pastel fabrics if they are arranged in clusters. Intersecting bands can be added to your design to set off or separate the units as shown in Color Plates 7 and 10.

DESIGN APPROACH 3 - MIRROR IMAGE

Like the beginning of the four-time repeat, you start this design approach using eight triangles, two of each of your four fabrics. Arrange them into a small square unit. Next, try to visualize holding a mirror on its side to the right side of this unit. If you did, the unit would reflect in the mirror, and a second unit would appear, only in reverse order.

To get the two bottom units of the mirror image again imagine holding a mirror on its side along the bottom edge of the two constructed units. If you looked into the mirror you would see a total of four units, or the arrangement shown. The two bottom units are just a reversal of the top two units. See how this differs in appearance from the four-time repeat.

Color Plate 3 shows a good arrangement of the mirror image in contrasting colors. Color Plate 5 shows vivid coloring with intersecting bands, while Color Plate 4 illustrates another design possibility this approach offers when executed in soft, delicate coloring.

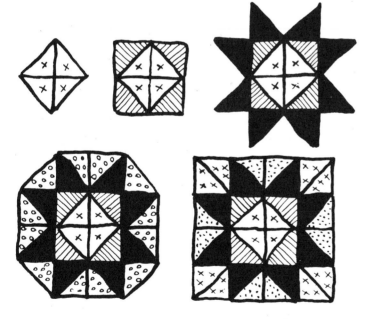

DESIGN APPROACH 4 - STAR DESIGN

Many interesting and beautiful star designs can evolve from your basic triangle patches. Color Plates 8 and 9 show two variations. To start a star, join four triangles to form a square. Add four more triangles onto the sides of the square as shown. Next, form the eight star points, choosing your most dominant fabric, either a very bold or bright print, or perhaps the lightest of your fabrics.

Study Color Plates 8 and 9 to notice the slight variation in the placement of fabrics. The pillow in Color Plate 9 was finished into an octagon shape. If you eliminate the four outside corner patches, the octagon shape results.

Use the remainder of your triangles to fill in around the star points.

OTHER DESIGN VARIATIONS

The four discussed design approaches are only a few of the many possibilities you can develop from your triangle shapes. Color Plates 12 and 13 show two pillow designs, each consisting of four different fabrics and each arranged in totally different compositions. The pillow in Color Plate 12 is done with vibrant fabrics of three color families, while Color Plate 13 shows a pillow very much the

opposite. Its fabrics are pastels and the arrangement is in four groups as in a mirror image, but with some switching of fabric placement. Notice how the ruffle adds softness to the design's outside shape.

The Chevron stripe design in Color Plate 14 is composed of two different prints. This striking coverlet was done by a young high school student as her first quilt or coverlet. Many other design variations can be achieved with the Chevron stripe. 11

Assembling Sequence

When you purchase a commercial dress pattern, an instruction sheet is usually enclosed telling you not so much how to sew, but giving you the suggested sequence of assembling the garment. Patchwork patterns, on the other hand, usually won't give you this detailed information; but with a little practice and thought you can quickly learn the sequence of assembling any block or pattern. We suggest a few basic rules.

Rule 1

Always lay your total design or block out in front of you before assembling. This gives you a good chance to study the patches and decide on their assembling sequence. It will also eliminate your chances of picking up the wrong patches and sewing them together, which will often happen if you have your patches stacked in a pile.

To make your design or block more portable, arrange the patches on a clean cookie sheet or on stiff cardboard, so you can put it away (perhaps under a bed or on top of the refrigerator) until you have time to work on the block again. You will find a cookie sheet easy to hold on your lap if you are watching television or set on the seat next to you if no table top is available.

Rule 2

Assemble patches into squares, blocks, stripes or units. Repeat this to yourself several times, then look at your design layout and see how this rule would apply. The drawings on this page will help explain the right and wrong choices you might make.

See pages 28, 30, 55, 70, and 71 for other examples of assembling sequence.

RIGHT   WRONG

RIGHT   WRONG

To incorporate bands into a patchwork design, assemble patchwork into units, then cut bands 1½'' to 2½'' wide. The length of the band is the same as the length of the unit.

Plate 1. Basic pillow with strong horizontal movement showing bold use of color. By JoAnn Shapiro.

Plate 2. Slanting diamond design utilizing basic triangle shapes. Bands, consisting of two fabrics, set off the design. By Donna Swenson.

Plate 3. A mirror image design using three fabrics and a corded edging. By Valerie Rudaitis.

Plate 4. Pastel fabrics are blended successfully into a mirror image. A fabric ruffle with lace on top sets off the design. By Cookie Lyou.

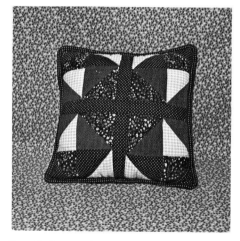

Plate 5. Intersecting bands give variety to this mirror image. By Nancy Fisher.

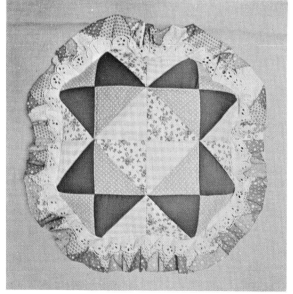

Plate 6. Colors chosen for this pillow front were suggested by the patchwork print purchased for the ruffle. By Helen Eltiste.

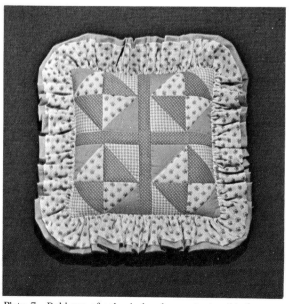

Plate 7. Bold use of color in bands punctuates this four-way repeat. Notice the good width of ruffle in relation to the inner design. By Sharline Hendrickson.

13

Hand Piecing

Before hand sewing, gather together the supplies you will need: Needles (assorted sharps are suggested), dressmaker's pins, sharp scissors, thread to match your fabric and dressmaker's beeswax.

For hand sewing cut your thread 18 inches long. This short thread will help eliminate the thread wearing and constantly breaking. A quick way to measure 18 inches is to cut the thread the same length as the distance from your elbow to your finger tips.

Using dressmaker's beeswax to wax your thread is beneficial for hand sewing in several ways. It strengthens the thread by coating the fibers, thus preventing dirt and soot from working into the fibers and wearing or weakening them. It also helps eliminate the tangling or twisting of your thread while doing hand sewing.

To wax your thread, pull your 18 inch strand across the surface of the wax about two times. Run your fingers down the thread to remove excess wax, and you are ready to go. Waxing for hand sewing is a must, so if you forget to do it and you are already sewing, just pull your needle free, wax the thread and put the needle back on again. After seeing its benefits, students often wax their thread whenever they do any hand sewing, such as buttons, hems, etc.

Having decided the sequence of assembling, lay your patches or design out in front of you. Choose two patches that should be joined together and place them right sides together. Pin them, once at the far left corner where the pencil lines meet, once in the middle, and once again on the right side where your lines meet. Check the back side of the two patches to see that the pins appear on the pencil lines in exactly the same place as on the front.

Right-handed people generally sew from right to left, and left-handed people from left to right. In either case, the hand stitch is the same. With a knot on the end of your thread, take a small stitch at the far right side of your two pinned patches. Left-handed people would be doing the same thing only starting on the far left side. Next take a small back stitch followed by two running stitches. Continue sewing in this manner (a back and two running, a back and two running) following on the pencil line across the patch until the left fabric edge is reached. To finish off your thread, take a backstitch, slipping your needle through the loop just before the thread pulls tight.

Remove pins as you reach them, giving your thread less to tangle around. Try to stitch eight to ten stitches per running inch. Some students find this awkward, but realize they have picked up speed after ten minutes or so.

Be sure to hand piece your first pillow project so that you will have a good chance to master the hand stitch. The basic triangle shape is an easy shape to sew, and it will let you concentrate on your stitching.

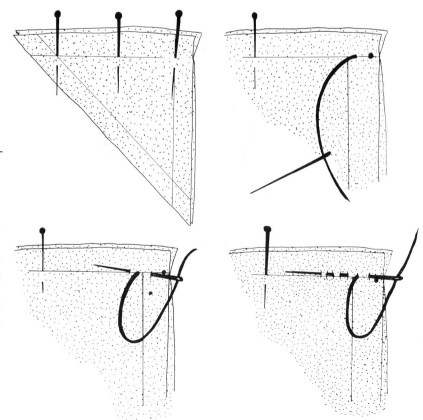

The Whys and Hows of Quilting

Quilting adds depth and dimension to your patchwork. In quilts, it's important because it's the stitching that holds the batting in place between the patchwork top and the back to make a warmer covering. In smaller objects, such as the pillow we are making, the tiny stitches of quilting add decoration. The light plays on the ridges and indentations made by the quilting stitches to further highlight the patchwork.

Basically, quilting is nothing more than a simple running stitch, done by hand, through three layers (pieced top, batting, and backing fabric). Quilting by machine is also possible; however, we prefer hand quilting because it gives a softness that can't be achieved by machine. If you feel you must try machine quilting for later projects, practice first to see if you really like it.

TYPES OF QUILTING DESIGNS

There are a number of design possibilities with quilting stitches -- you are limited only by your imagination. The designs can range from very simple outline quilting to very elaborate traditional designs.

Outline quilting is done by quilting parallel to the seam lines of the patchwork pieces. You can quilt to the inside or outside of the seams. This is probably one of the easiest and most popular quilting designs and is best for highlighting geometric shapes and designs.

Pictorial quilting can be used very successfully to highlight a scene. The sketch of House On A Hill shows how quilting gives new highlights to the basic block by creating clouds and smoke in the sky, etc. You could add some interesting details of your own.

There are also many traditional quilting designs that you can purchase or will find in books and magazines. These designs are usually hearts, flowers, scrolls, etc. and can be very elaborate. Usually, designs such as these will not show up clearly on patterned fabric and are best if saved for plain colors.

MARKING THE PILLOW TOP FOR QUILTING

For the pillow project, you will probably be most comfortable doing outline quilting. It requires little or no marking on the pillow top -- you simply quilt ¼" to 1/8" parallel to the seam line. If you want to make a certain area stand out, quilting around the outside of it will give it a slight puff.

You probably will be able to "eyeball" a quilting line for outline quilting, but if you feel you can't follow parallel to the seam line and keep your quilting stitches straight, you may want to mark on the pillow top. There are a number of ways to do this. One is to lay masking tape on the pillow top with the edge of the tape right along the line where you want to quilt. Another way is to take a ruler and draw a line parallel to the seam line of the block using a hard lead pencil, soap sliver, or dressmaker's pencil.

If you would like to add a quilting design such as a flower or heart to some of the plain triangles in your pillow top, you could make a template of the shape you want and pencil lightly around it. Another approach would be to use Saral paper or dressmaker's carbon and use it as you would carbon paper to apply your design. Be sure to test any method you choose for washability.

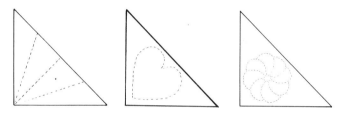

Some ideas for quilting triangles

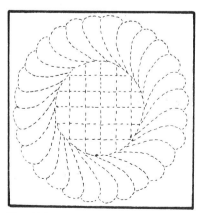

Traditional Quilting

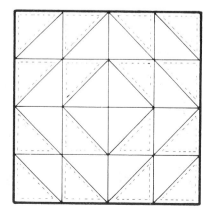

Outline Quilting

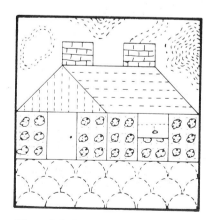

Pictorial Quilting

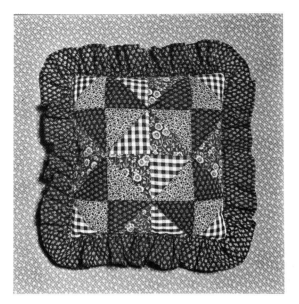

Plate 8. A monochromatic selection of fabrics produces this stunning star pattern. By Pat McAlearney.

Plate 9. The basic triangle shapes, made in fabrics from two color families, produce this bold star pattern. By Kathy Haas.

Plate 10. Bold orange bands, with matching ruffle, separate the basic pillow into four visual units. By Louellen Sweinhart.

Plate 11. Narrow bands, seamed to triangles of the same fabric, appear to merge in the edge of the design. By Angela Samson.

Plate 12. Clever use of four fabrics in the basic triangle creates the illusion of an eight-pointed star. By Fujiko Yamasaki.

Plate 13. The basic triangle, executed in soft pastels, makes this nicely balanced pillow top. By Sally Barnum.

Plate 14. Two fabrics cut in the basic triangle have been cleverly combined to form this Chevron Stripe coverlet. By Nancy Andrews.

Plate 15. Pillow backs in a pleasing arrangement.

Plate 16. A four-piece back is done in two fabrics.

Plate 17. Six-piece monochromatic back, accented by a lighter ruffle.

Plate 18. A pleasing balance of four fabrics in three colors. Smaller pieces of fabric can be combined for a back such as this. See Plate 12 for the front of this pillow.

Plate 19. Bands and ruffle of the same red print give balance to this four-piece back. See Plate 20 for the front of this pillow.

Plate 16. By Angela Samson.

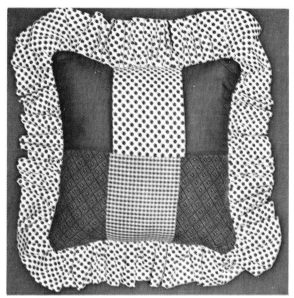

Plate 17. By Susan Bennett.

Plate 18. By Fujiko Yamasaki.

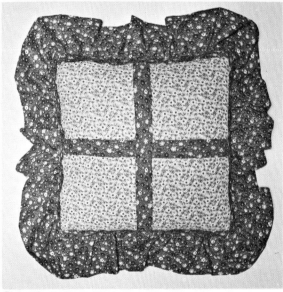

Plate 19. By Jessie Hoyt.

THE LAYERS

Patchwork Pillow Front

Once you have finished piecing your pillow front and have marked your quilting design where necessary, you are ready to combine it with the batting and backing fabric which make up the "sandwich" you will quilt through.

Batting

For this project, purchase bonded polyester sheet batting rather than cotton, which tends to shread and lump. This is designed for quiltmaking and is bonded into a sheet-type roll. It differs from polyester "stuffing" in that it doesn't pull apart easily and will remain in place when you use it for projects like this one or in a quilt. Batting comes in different thicknesses -- from very thin that would be good for placemats to very thick, which is ideal for tied comforters. Batting that is about ½" thick is best for this project -- thicker batting could make your quilting more difficult. If you find that the batting is slightly irregular in places, thicker or thinner in spots, pass a warm steam iron over it and you can make it more uniform.

Backing

In the case of this pillow, the backing fabric will be hidden on the inside of the pillow, so now is the time to use up any fabric you have on hand that would be easy to quilt through. If this project were a quilt, this would be the back of the quilt and you would purchase fabric that would coordinate with the quilt. A lightweight cotton or cotton/polyester blend will be best. An old sheet will work fine for this fabric, but some sheets have a very high thread count and this makes it more difficult to quilt through; so be aware of this when choosing your fabric. Preshrink the fabric and iron it free of any major wrinkles.

ASSEMBLING THE SANDWICH

Once you have collected the three layers (pieced top, batting and backing fabric), you are ready to assemble the "sandwich". Cut your backing fabric and batting one inch larger on all sides than your pieced pillow top. For example, if your pillow top is 14" square, cut the batting and backing fabric each 16" square. This extra allows for any take up in these layers during the quilting. Nothing is more frustrating than cutting all layers the same and then trying to keep everything exactly even as you quilt. The batting and backing fabric have a natural tendency to pull in slightly. Any excess that hasn't pulled in during quilting will be trimmed off later.

On a flat, firm surface, such as a hardwood floor or a table top (not the carpeting or your lap), place the backing fabric down first (right or wrong side won't matter). Next place a layer of the batting on top of the backing fabric. Smooth out any bumps and even up these two layers. Now place the pieced patchwork top on these two layers with the right side facing you. Be sure you have centered it so that about 1" of the batting and backing is showing on all sides.

Beginning in the center and working out in all directions, pin the three layers together carefully and make sure you haven't caused any major wrinkles in the batting or backing fabric.

Now you are ready to baste the three layers together. The basting stitches can be large, about 1" to 1½". Baste from edge to edge in both directions and diagonally as in the illustration. Once you have done this, baste around the edges. This will hold the layers together as you quilt.

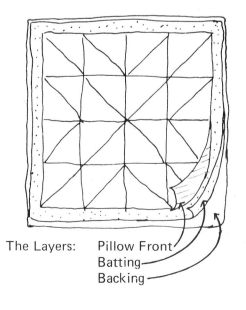

The Layers: Pillow Front
Batting
Backing

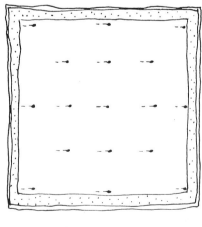

Pinning the layers

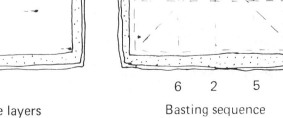

Basting sequence

QUILTING

Most people prefer to use a short, strong needle for quilting (a no. 7 or 8 quilting or between). Longer needles, which tend to be thinner, will often bend when used for quilting. As you become more experienced, you will decide what needle works best for you.

Running stitch for quilting

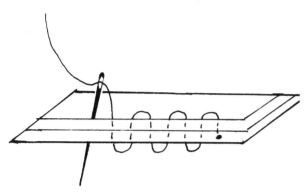

Hiding the beginning knot when quilting

Thread your needle with 18 inches of single thickness quilting or heavy duty thread. Quilting thread is "pre-waxed" with a silicone coating. You may also use regular sewing thread, but if you do, wax it with dressmaker's beeswax to prevent tangling and knotting.

The color of thread is up to you. Choose one that coordinates well with your project. Keep in mind that if you choose a color that contrasts greatly with your pillow top, your quilting stitches will be more noticeable -- a feature you might like better after you've had more experience quilting.

Quilt, according to your design, by beginning in the center of your pillow front and work toward all edges. To do this, knot one end of the thread and bring the needle up from the back through all three layers. Give an extra tug on the thread so that the knot will pull through the backing fabric and hide in the batting. Even though the back of your quilting will not show on this pillow, this is a good time to practice this technique. Take a backstitch to secure your thread and begin to quilt with a running stitch. Try to have about six to eight stitches per inch showing on the pillow front. Usually, you will be able to take about two running stitches at a time. Some quilters can get eight stitches on a needle at once, but that takes practice! The amount of stitches you can get on the needle and the number of stitches you take per inch will be determined by various factors such as your experience with quilting, the thickness of the batting, the type of fabric, and sometimes your mood.

Don't worry about what the back of your quilting looks like this time -- it won't show. Use this pillow top as a chance to practice. When you get to other projects where the quilting will show on the back, you will want to hide all knots and have all stitches, front and back, look even.

Trim away the excess batting and backing fabric even with the pillow front.

Plate 20. Three pillows from the basic triangle show how patchwork can add color and interest to any setting. From left by Daisy Hughes, Pat Christy, and Jessie Hoyt.

Plate 21. Patchwork, clay, wood, weaving, and applique combine in this natural setting. From left by Susan Bennett, Lois Jensen (center), and Chris Hammerschmidt.

Plate 22. Fabric ruffle with gathered eyelet on top. By Pat Christy.

Plate 23. A double ruffle with lace top stitched on fold of the fabric ruffle. By Wilma Maddock.

Plate 24. Two fabrics combined in a double ruffle. By Susan Bennett.

Plate 25. A double ruffle and lace give a three-tiered effect. By Sally Barnum.

Plate 26. Lace is top stitched to the edge of the fabric ruffle and pillow top. By Judy Johnson.

Plate 22.

Plate 26.

Plate 23.

Plate 25.

Plate 24.

Types of Edgings and Ruffles

Edge trimmings enhance pillows and give them a professional look. Two of the most popular types of edge trims are cording (or piping) and ruffles. In this section you will learn how to do a gathered fabric ruffle.

There are many types of ruffles including those with gathered or ungathered eyelet, double or triple ruffles of fabric and/or lace, and fabric ruffles with lace attached to the free edge of the ruffle. The pillows in Color Plates 22 through 26 illustrate the many variations. All give the pillow a nice, finished look.

CALCULATING FABRIC FOR A RUFFLE

In order to determine how much fabric to buy for the ruffle, you will need to know how wide and how long you are going to make it.

Width. Fabric ruffles are made double thickness with the fold on the outside edge so they have a finished look on both sides. First, decide how wide you would like the ruffle to be. You will need to double that measurement and then add a seam allowance to each edge.

> Example: If you have chosen a 3-inch ruffle, you will need to cut your strips of fabric 7 inches wide to provide for a double thickness of fabric and two ½-inch seam allowances.

Length. To determine the length of material you will need for a ruffle with a good amount of fullness, consider the following points:

(1) For medium-weight fabrics such as cotton blends, the length of ruffle should be 2½ times the distance around the pillow front.

(2) Heavy fabrics require less fullness -- about 1½ to 2 times the distance around the pillow will be sufficient.

(3) Light-weight fabrics require more fullness to look good. Make them 3 times the distance around the pillow.

(4) If you are making multiple fabric ruffles (two or more fabrics gathered together in one ruffle), allow 1½ times the distance around the pillow for each fabric.

(5) Narrow ruffles require less fabric than do wide ones.

You won't be able to buy fabric that is wide enough to allow you to cut one strip of fabric and have it be enough for the ruffle, so you will probably need to cut two or more strips across the fabric. The example on the following page will help you determine the number of strips to cut.

(Note: The following is an <u>example</u> of calculating the amount of fabric for a ruffle. Please adjust these calculations using the measurement of your pillow.)

<u>Example:</u> To make a nice full ruffle of medium-weight fabric for a pillow that measures 40 inches around (10 inches on each side), you could cut two and one-half strips across a 45 inch piece of fabric. That would give you about 110 inches of fabric to work with once you have seamed the strips together (or almost three times the measurement of the pillow).

Purchasing Fabric for Ruffle. To calculate the exact amount of fabric to purchase, decide how many strips across the fabric you will need to cut and how wide the strips will be. In the two previous examples, we decided to cut two and one-half strips, each 7 inches wide. That means we will need three 7 inch widths, or 21 inches of fabric that is 45 inches wide (half of one strip will be left over). Therefore, 5/8 yards of fabric should be purchased for the ruffle in our example.

On some occasions, you will have a piece of fabric for the ruffle that has a stripe or other pattern running lengthwise. If you want to take advantage of the stripes and cut the strips for the ruffle lengthwise, it will require just a little more piecing. You might want to purchase more fabric and have fewer strips to piece - just save the leftover fabric for other patchwork.

MAKING THE RUFFLE

Cut the ruffle fabric the length and width you will need, piecing the strips where necessary to make one continuous loop of fabric. Fold this loop in half lengthwise with <u>wrong sides together.</u> <u>Divide the fabric length into fourths and mark these points with safety pins on the folded edge.</u>

Gathering the Ruffle. A good way to gather this ruffle is to cut a long piece of strong or double thread and knot it in one end. Bring it through the ruffle fabric in the seam allowance. <u>Lay the thread inside the seam allowance parallel to the raw edge and sew over it with a zig-zag stitch.</u> Be careful not to sew through the thread. This zig-zag stitch will form a casing over the thread, and it will gather the ruffle very nicely when pulled. <u>Don't pull the gathering thread until you attach the ruffle to the pillow front.</u>

If you use the traditional method of gathering where you sew two rows of large stitches on the sewing machine and pull the bobbin threads, then start and stop each row where you have marked the divisions of the ruffle in fourths. This will make it easier to gather the sections and the threads are not as likely to break.

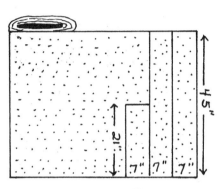

Bolt of fabric for ruffle

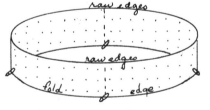

Safety pins dividing ruffle length into fourths.

A casing has been formed by machine zig-zag stitching over a strong gathering thread.

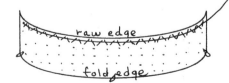

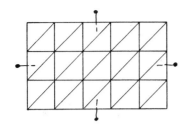

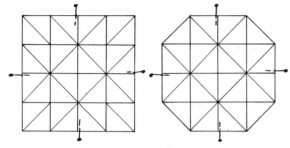

Dividing the pillow front into fourths

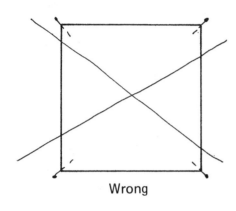

Wrong

ATTACHING THE RUFFLE

Divide the pillow front into fourths and mark these divisions with safety pins or straight pins. The middle of each edge would be a good place to mark as you see in these examples.

Pin the ruffle to the pillow front, matching the raw edges of the ruffle and pillow. The safety pins that divided the ruffle into fourths should be at the same position on the pillow as the pins that divided the pillow front as you will see in the illustration at the bottom of the page. Draw up the gathering thread on the ruffle to meet the pillow front, spacing the gathers evenly and allowing extra fullness at the corners. Machine baste the ruffle to the pillow front with a ½ inch seam allowance.

After stitching, check to make sure that the folded edge of the ruffle didn't get caught at the corners or any other place. Keep the ruffle flat against the pillow front as you join the back to it. A good way might be to lightly baste the folded edge of the ruffle to the pillow top so that it doesn't get caught when the back is stitched in place.

RUFFLE VARIATIONS

Once you have mastered the basic ruffle, the variations can be easily applied.

Multiple Fabric Ruffles. Multiple fabric or fabric and lace ruffles where one fabric is wider than the other are very attractive. For example, one ruffle could be 5-inches wide with a 3-inch ruffle in front of it, or combine a 3-inch and a 1½-inch ruffle. To make these, simply prepare each loop of fabric for the ruffle as in the preceding section. Place the narrow ruffle on top of the wide one with the raw edges matching when putting in the gathering stitches. Gather them at the same time, and they will be less bulky to sew through and manipulate.

Lace. To put lace on the free edge of the ruffle, sew narrow lace by hand or machine to the free edge of the ungathered ruffle fabric.

Trim. After the pillow is completed, trim or small laces can be hand applied to the pillow.

Pregathered Eyelet. To use pregathered eyelet as a ruffle, purchase enough eyelet for the measurement around the pillow plus 10 inches for joining the free edges of the eyelet together and turning the corners. Apply this to the pillow top in the same manner as you would for a fabric ruffle. Be sure to allow extra fullness at the corners by taking little pleats, using about 1½ inches in each corner.

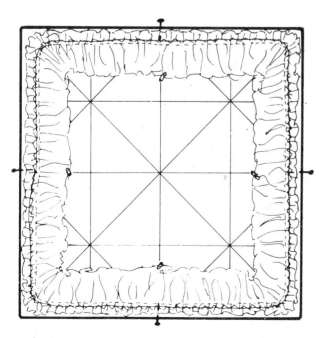

Gathering the ruffle to fit the pillow front

PREPARING THE PILLOW BACK

Designing the back of the pillow gives you another chance to be creative. The back doesn't need to be just one piece of fabric. Experiment with some of the following ideas or create some of your own. (Color Plates 15 - 19)

(1) Use one piece of fabric, but quilt it in an interesting design.

(2) Make a simple patchwork design of squares or stripes of fabrics that you used in the front of the pillow.

(3) Patch squares of one or more of the fabrics and set them apart by bands of another fabric.

(4) Piece another front for a reversible pillow.

The size of the back must be the same size as the pillow front. Measure the front and make yourself a paper pattern exactly the same size and shape. This will automatically include the seam allowance for the edge. If you decide to divide the back into any type of patchwork, you will need to add seam allowances to every piece you cut, so that when you join the sections together, they will make the finished pillow back the size you need.

To do this, make another paper pattern, drawing the outside shape. With a second color of ink, draw in the divisions you want. When you cut this apart for your individual patterns, add a seam allowance to each edge that has the second color of ink on it. Cut and sew the fabrics together with the seam allowance you have added. Compare the finished piece with your original pattern to be sure it is the right size.

When you have completed the pillow back, you may want to quilt it. If so, prepare it in the same way you did the front by making a sandwich with batting and a backing fabric. Baste and quilt, then trim any excess batting and lining fabric.

JOINING THE BACK OF THE PILLOW TO THE FRONT

Once you have machine basted with the ruffled edge machine basted to the front of the pillow, place the back of the pillow on top of it so that the right sides are facing. Pin them a few times on each edge. Now flip this over and stitch to the left side of the machine basting stitches that are showing. By doing this, you will be sure that your first row of stitches won't show when you turn the pillow. Be careful that you don't catch the free edge of the ruffle in this seam. If you basted it down carefully, this shouldn't happen. Leave an opening on one of the sides that is about ¾ of the length of that side so that you will have plenty of room to stuff the pillow. Backstitch when you start and stop the stitching so it won't come loose when you stuff the pillow.

Trim the corners and turn the pillow inside out. Unbaste the ruffle and it should stand out nicely. Check all of the edges carefully to be sure that all seam allowances have been caught into the seam and the free edges of the ruffle didn't get caught anywhere. Now is the time to fix anything.

STUFFING THE PILLOW

The supplies you will need for stuffing the pillow are polyester sheet batting (the same as you used for quilting the pillow top) and polyester stuffing or fiberfill (the loose stuff that isn't bonded into a sheet).

A good way to get a nice smooth pillow with a minimum of lumps is to make a "pillowcase" out of the polyester batting. To do this, cut a piece of batting the width of the pillow and twice the length. Fold it in the middle and hand whipstitch (or lace) the two sides together, leaving the end opposite the fold open. Be sure not to sew this batting pillowcase on the sewing machine as that will give a hard ridge. When you put your hand into the whipped edge, you will see how it curls and butts up against itself to make a smooth edge. Insert this pillowcase into your pillow, matching up the corners and opening.

Now you are ready to stuff the inside of the "pillowcase" with the polyester stuffing. This is not a fast job and should not be treated as such. Work with the stuffing by pulling it apart and fluffing it as you are getting ready to put it in the cavity. Work with a handful at a time. If you are putting the stuffing into the cavity with your right hand, knead the pillow from the outside with the left hand to help manipulate the stuffing into a nice shape. Pack the stuffing into the corners with the end of a wooden spoon and then work it in rows across the pillow. It is a lot easier to smooth out lumps now while you can manipulate the stuffing from the inside and outside.

Continue to stuff the pillow until you like the thickness and then stuff it some more! This is because the stuffing will tend to settle as you use the pillow. When the pillow is sufficiently stuffed, pin the opening shut and slipstitch it closed.

CLEANING AND LAUNDERING THE FINISHED PILLOW

Here are some suggestions for keeping your pillow clean and fresh looking. You might want to Scotchguard it. If you have found some surface dirt, you could try to lightly sponge it clean.

The pillow can always be opened where you slipstitched it closed and the stuffing removed before laundering by hand. Roll it up in a towel for ten to fifteen minutes to remove the excess water and leave it to dry. You can fluff it up by placing it in a dryer set on the "air" or no heat cycle with a hot, wrungout wet towel for ten to fifteen minutes.

Hexagons And Other Hand Pieced Patterns

DESIGN AND COLOR VARIATIONS

The six-sided or hexagon shape is one of the earliest patterns recorded in patchwork. The Grandmother's Flower Garden design is probably the most often seen arrangement. Another stunning arrangement is the Mosaic or Honeycomb. The Wave pattern gives the patchwork student still another opportunity to experiment and create an interesting flow of color. Don't let your imagination stop with these examples. Try some of the other designs shown on the next page and feel free to try out your own ideas.

Carefully consider your fabrics, their colors and prints before planning an arrangement of hexagons. (Color Plate 27, 28). Mixing many printed fabrics will give your finished work a warm richness often not seen in the quickly constructed quilts of today. As your own designer, you can control the feel your patchwork item evokes. For a soft or aged look, experiment with the wrong side of your fabrics. (Color Plate 30). Combining the wrong and right sides also has the advantage of doubling the amount of fabrics at your disposal. Contemporary looking items will result when you combine bold or bright colors.

Hexagonal patchwork is an ideal way to use up small scraps of various prints or colors, as no definite repeat of any one fabric is necessary.

Grandmother's Flower Garden

Random arrangement

Wave pattern

Hexagons arranged in strips

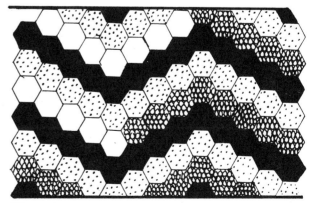

Wave pattern

BEAUTIFULLY DESIGNED ARRANGEMENTS OF HEXAGONS

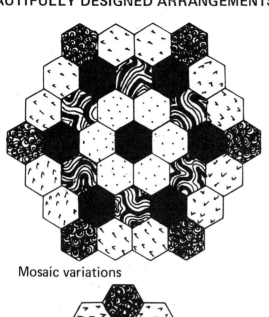

Mosaic variations

Star pattern

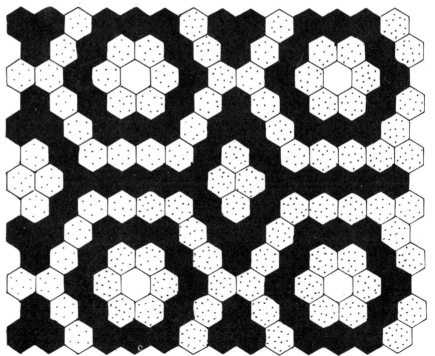

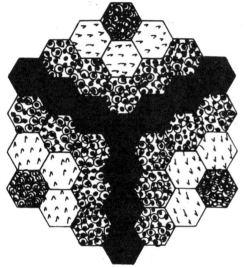

Diamond pattern

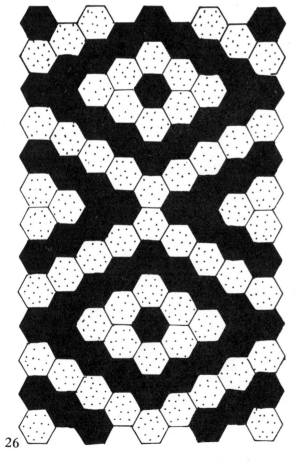

Stepping Stones

Hexagons
Seven Sizes

1"
1¼"
1½"
1¾"
2"
2¼"
2½"

TEMPLATE MAKING, TRACING ONTO THE FABRIC

Seven hexagon pattern sizes ranging from 1 inch to 2½ inches are given above. When a hexagon shape or template is referred to as being 1 inch in size, it is meant that any one of its six sides will measure 1 inch long. For your first experience with hexagons, use the 1½ inch size. You will also want to trace the next larger size, or the 1¾ inch hexagon. This second size will be your pattern for a built-in seam allowance of ¼ inch.

If you were constructing a large patchwork item, such as a quilt or table cover, you would want to make several sturdy templates of each of the two sizes. In this case you would want to have on hand approximately five of both the 1½ inch and 1¾ inch hexagon templates. As you trace around the templates preparing the eight hundred or more that might be needed for a large project, the corners on the template will soften. When this occurs replace it with a new template. Be sure that all of the templates of one size are exactly the same and that each of the six sides of the template are the same length.

Two methods are commonly used to prepare and assemble the hexagons. Both are described on the following pages and we suggest to students that they try both methods to find the one most suitable for them.

SUITABLE FABRICS

Choose from firmly woven, pure cotton or cotton polyester fabrics for your first attempt. Do not mix fabrics of different weights, and be sure that all of your fabrics have been preshrunk and ironed smooth. Stay away from transparent fabrics such as voile or dotted swiss. These fabrics are so sheer that the seam allowance, when pushed to the back side, will show through. Leave knits and pile fabrics such as velvet, corduroy or uncut corduroy alone for your first attempts with the hexagon shape. The experienced patchwork craftsman wishing to experiment with these bulky fabrics should choose the 2 inch or larger pattern pieces. Keep this in mind when you want to do a quilt or large project on the sewing machine. The larger hexagon shape is easier to assemble by machine than the smaller one.

Hexagons - Method 1

Method 1 - Using a Paper Core: Using a sharp pencil, trace around the outside edge of your 1½ inch template on medium-weight paper. A grocery bag or shelf paper is ideal, while notebook paper or newspaper is too thin. You will need one paper hexagon shape for each fabric hexagon. Cut the paper shapes carefully and be sure their sides are smooth, accurate in length and free of jags. These can be stacked and set aside.

Trace your 1¾ inch template onto the <u>wrong side</u> of your fabrics. This larger size template will give you a ¼ inch seam allowance and will finish into the 1½ inch size. The grain of the fabric should run parallel to any one edge of your template. Trace and cut carefully all of the fabric shapes you will need. Center and pin one paper shape onto the wrong side of a fabric hexagon. Finger press the ¼ inch seam allowance over the paper and baste in place. At the corners fold over the seam allowance, making the corners sharp and accurate. Your basting can be done with or without a knot. Baste around the patch using one or two stitches to carry you across a side. Your basting stitches need to be smaller at the corners. Finish off your work by taking a small stitch in place, then remove the pins and prepare the next fabric and paper core hexagon. Leave the basting in place until the hexagons are assembled. You may press the shapes lightly with a steam iron at this time if it is needed.

Accuracy is very important when sewing hexagons. We prefer hand sewing as it is the most accurate way of joining the patches. Lay your hexagons out into the design or shape you like best. You can then gather them up into groups, either planning to sew them together into rows or into rosettes. The paper core method is easiest to assemble into rosettes.

Place two patches right sides together. Sew one set of edges together using small, overcasting stitches. Sew a third patch into place. As you stitch it to the inside corner, sew two stitches in place both before and after you turn the corner. This will give you a firm, secure corner.

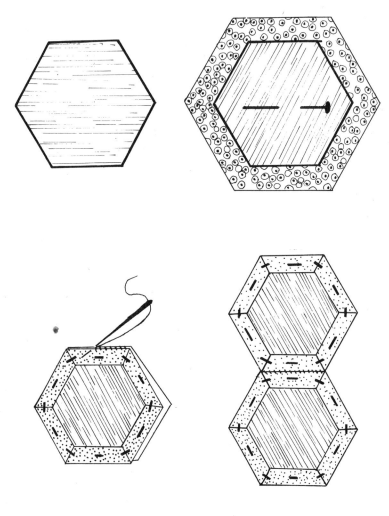

There are two methods for assembling hexagons. (1) When assembling a rosette, sew all hexagons around and out from one central hexagon. (2) You can also assemble hexagons in rows. Your basting can be removed when all the sides or edges of the hexagon are sewn in place. Many people choose to leave the paper core in the finished item.

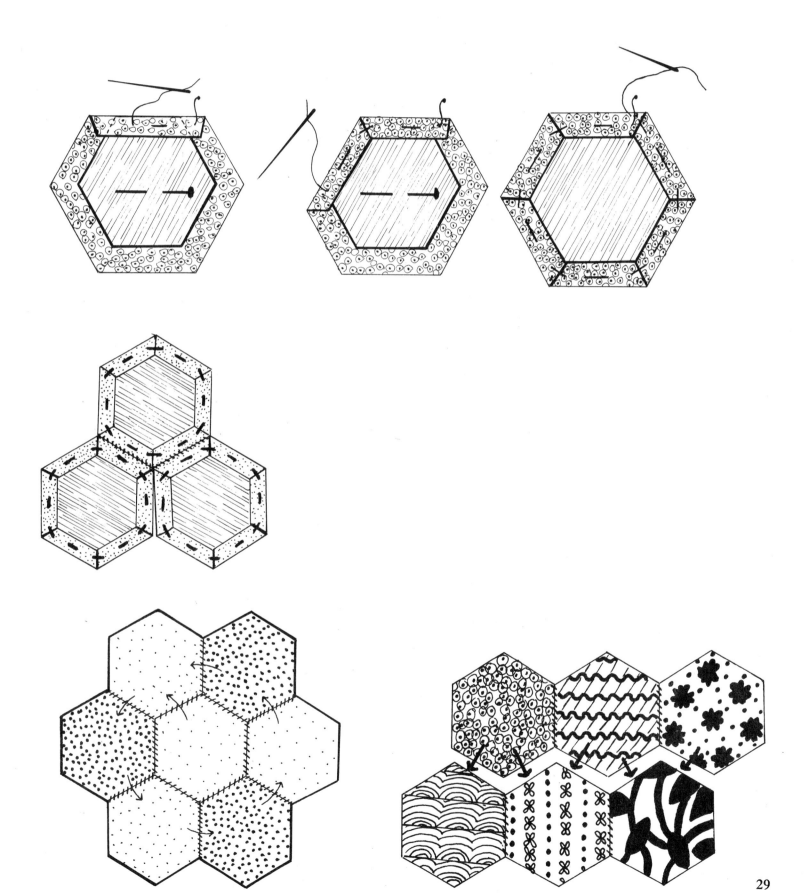

Hexagons - Method 2

Method 2 - Penciled-In Stitching Lines. Trace onto the <u>wrong side</u> of your fabric the larger of your two hexagon patterns. Repeat until you have all the hexagon shapes you need drawn. Do not cut these out yet. Center the smaller hexagon pattern over your tracing. Carefully trace around the small template. This second or inside pencil line will serve as a sewing line. It is easier to trace the smaller shape while the patch is still attached to your yardage. Cut the patches out with smooth, accurate strokes.

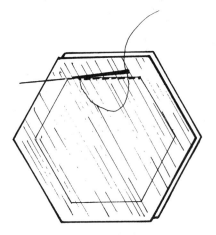

To assemble, place two patches with their <u>right sides together</u> and pin with two pins at the corners where the pencil lines meet. Hand stitch using the basic patchwork stitch (one back, two running) across the penciled line. Notice that the stitching starts at the pencil corners where you have your pins. Stitch only from one pencil line to the other, never from one fabric edge to the other

When you are setting a hexagon into an inside corner, take a backstitch just before the corner at the crossing seam and again immediately on the other side, or just after you have pivoted the corner. The finished results can't be surpassed for firmness and accuracy. The hexagons could also be assembled into rows instead of rosettes.

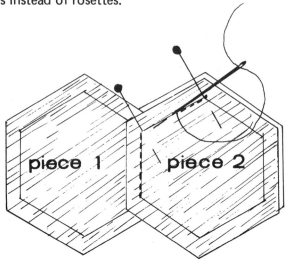

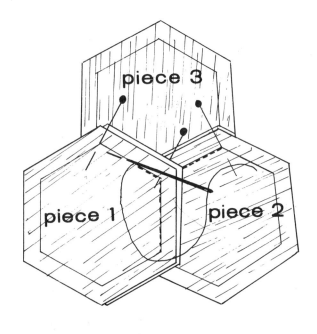

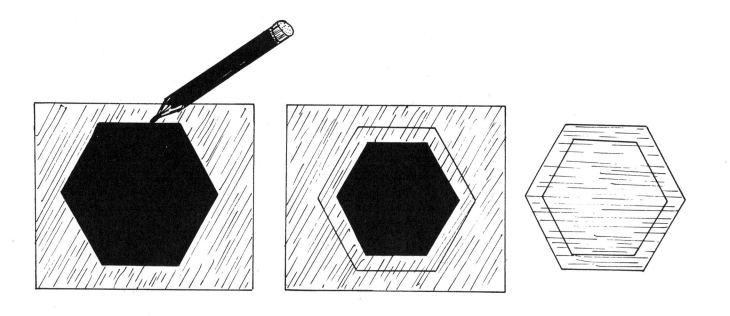

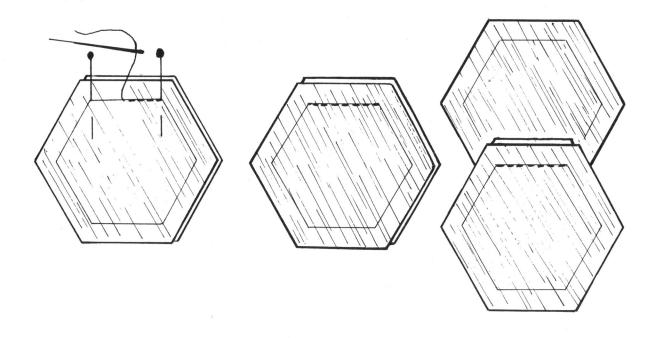

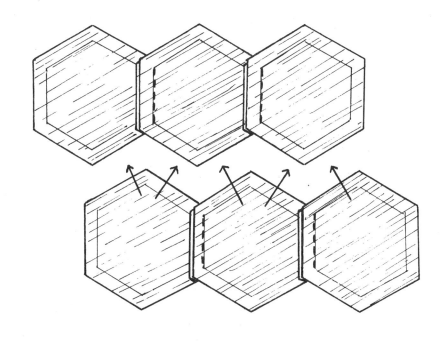

Quilting. Very little space is available within a hexagon to design an elaborate quilting design, so usually you will see quilting done following the contours of the individual hexagons.

Finishing. A single flower motif is attractive on a child's dress front, in the center of a pillow, or applied to the front or back of a work shirt as shown on the cover. In all of these suggested examples the rosette can be hand or machine appliqued in place. Don't overlook other possibilities, such as pincushions bench tops, seat covers, sleeves and yokes for caftans, and even coverlets.

Rolling Star

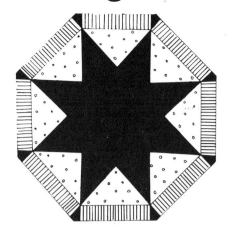

18" octagon

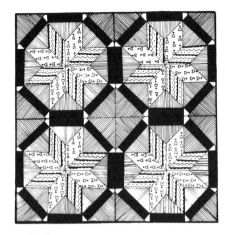

Repeat of four blocks

Repeat of four blocks

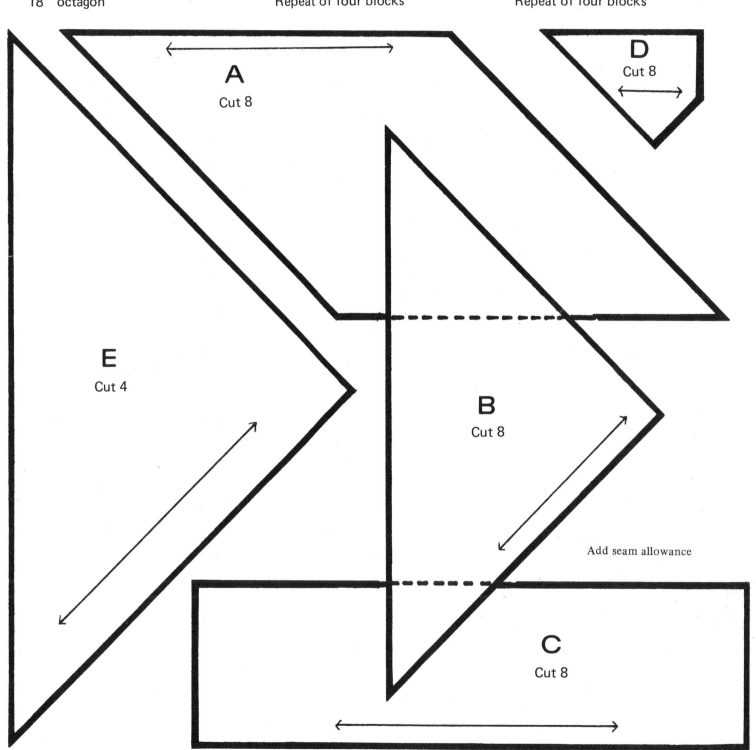

A
Cut 8

D
Cut 8

E
Cut 4

B
Cut 8

Add seam allowance

C
Cut 8

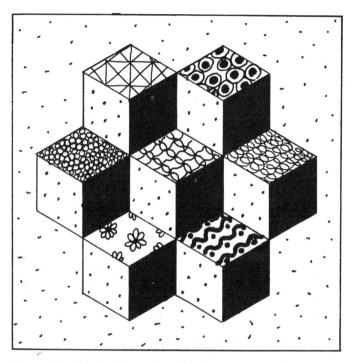

Seven blocks appliqued on fabric

Yardage of continuous blocks
See Color Plate on Page 37

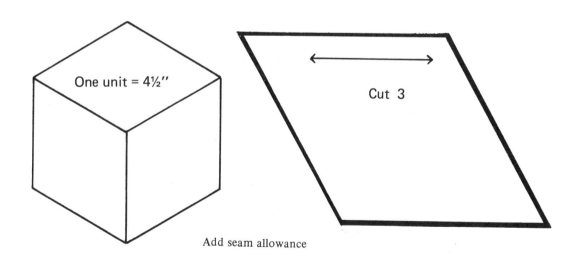

One unit = 4½"

Cut 3

Add seam allowance

Hexagon, Triangle, And Diamond

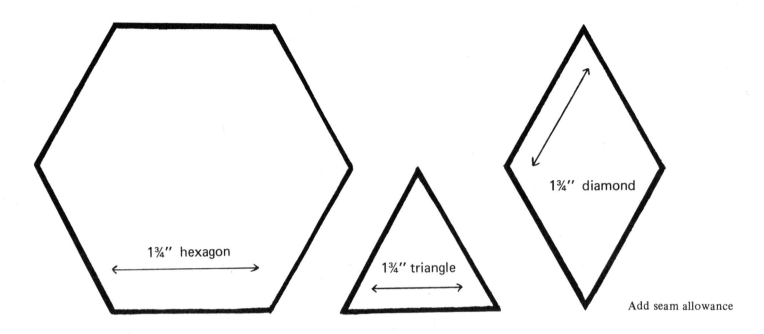

1¾'' hexagon

1¾'' triangle

1¾'' diamond

Add seam allowance

Because their sides are the same length
(1¾''), these three shapes can be combined
into a large variety of designs.

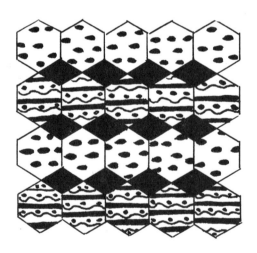

12" design

15" design

15" design

Kansas Dugout

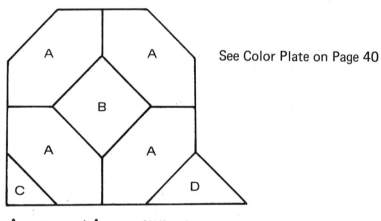

See Color Plate on Page 40

Arrangement A   4½" unit

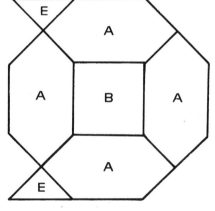

Arrangement B   5" unit

Add seam allowance

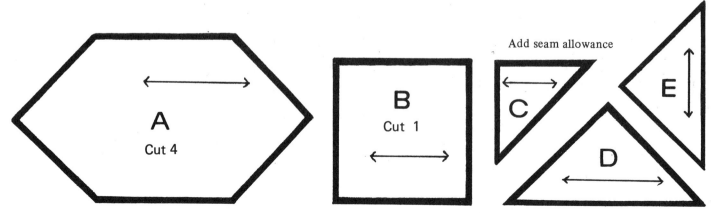

Plate 27. A random splattering of hexagons compose the sleeve and yoke of this caftan modeled by Donna Mullen. Designed by Diane Hubbs.

Plate 28. One large rosette of hexagons produced a striking table mat. By Trinette Shelton. The handbag was cut from fabric made by piecing hexagons in the rosette design. By Nancy Afonsky.

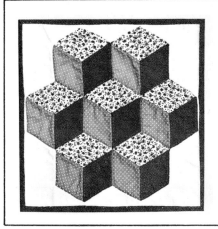

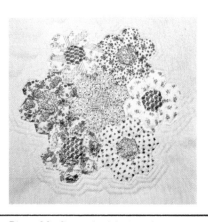

Plate 29. Seven Baby Blocks of three fabrics show vividly when appliqued to a white background. By Joan Beucke.

Plate 30. Seven hand pieced rosettes of hexagons were appliqued onto the background fabric. By Marjorie Puckett.

Plate 31. Another effect was achieved by constantly using different fabric for the third side of these baby blocks. By Lois Jensen.

Plate 32. This Jack's Chain quilt is an unusual example of combining squares, triangles and hexagons. By Lydia Davis. A Rail Fence skirt is modeled by Donna Mullen. Designed by Lila More.

Jack's Chain

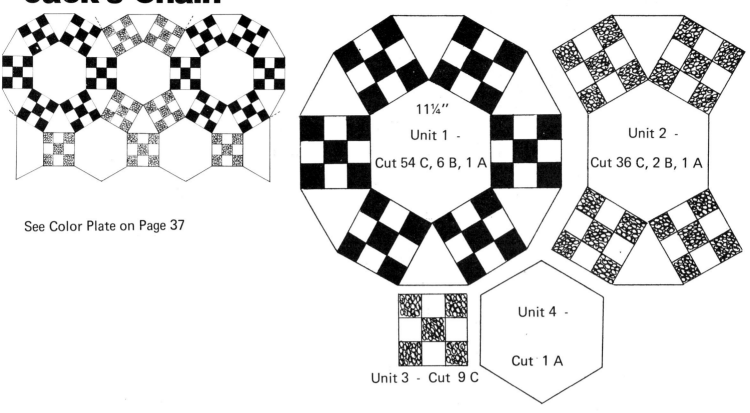

See Color Plate on Page 37

11¼"

Unit 1 -

Cut 54 C, 6 B, 1 A

Unit 2 -

Cut 36 C, 2 B, 1 A

Unit 4 -

Cut 1 A

Unit 3 - Cut 9 C

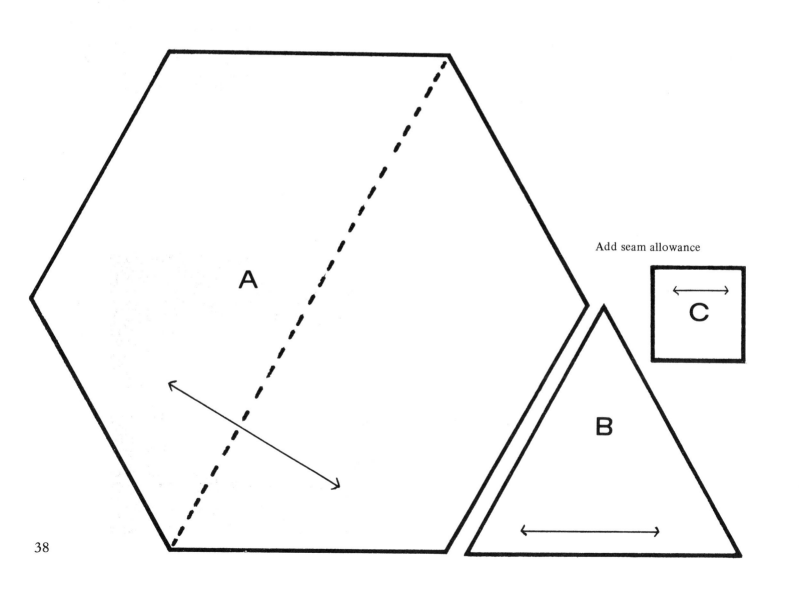

A

Add seam allowance

C

B

Mexican Rose

Repeat of four blocks

8'' square
See Color Plate on Page 40

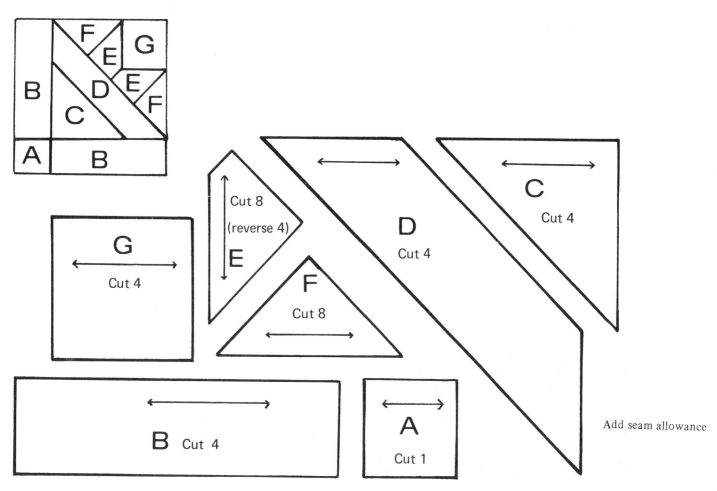

B

F
E
G
E
D
E
F
C
B

A
B

G
Cut 4

Cut 8
(reverse 4)
E

D
Cut 4

C
Cut 4

F
Cut 8

B   Cut 4

A
Cut 1

Add seam allowance

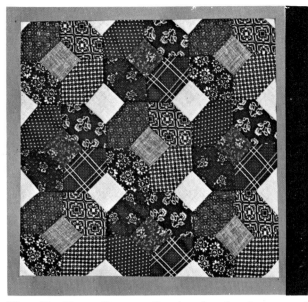

Plate 33. Kansas Dugout. By changing the placement of fabrics, two different patterns emerge. The variation on the right would be ideal for utilizing scraps. By Marjorie Puckett.

Plate 34. The intense colors of this Mexican Rose have been centralized by using a lighter fabric on the edges of the pattern. By Marjorie Puckett.

Plate 35. "Framed Square" is quick to cut and assemble and because of its overall size, adapts well to a variety of garments. By Marjorie Puckett.

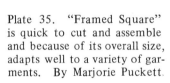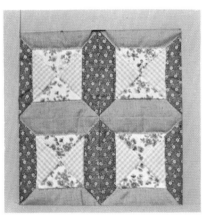

Plate 36. Patch pockets of Love-in-a-Mist add richness to this floor length jumper by Pat Porter. She further accented the bib top by taking the eight pieces from the center of the Love-in-a-Mist design. The Log Cabin design by Lila More adapts easily to a table cover, lap throw, wall hanging or bench pad.

Plate 37. Flying Geese and Goose Tracks. These two designs have been created using basically the same fabrics and pattern pieces. By Marjorie Puckett.

Plate 38. "Patience Corner" skirt consisting of double knit fabrics placed at random. By Gail Giberson.

Plate 39. This Log Cabin pillow consists of fabric strips arranged as opposites. By Myque Fisher. Background scrap coverlet by Marjorie Puckett.

Plate 40. A Log Cabin design can take on a contemporary appearance when two bold fabrics are combined in a spiral pattern. By Chris Hammerschmidt.

Plate 41. When doing the Card Trick pattern, a contrasting background fabric will help set off the four overlapping units. By Marjorie Puckett.

Flying Geese

13½" square

See Color Plate on Page 41

Repeat of four blocks

Design variations--repeat of four blocks

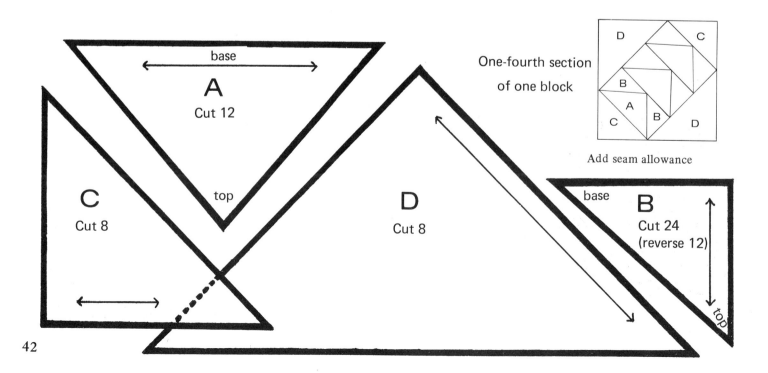

base

A

Cut 12

top

C

Cut 8

D

Cut 8

base

B

Cut 24
(reverse 12)

top

One-fourth section
of one block

D   C

B

A   B

C   D

Add seam allowance

42

Goose Tracks

Four rows of seven units each, separated by bands

See Color Plates on Pages 41 & 73

Four rows of six units each, separated by bands

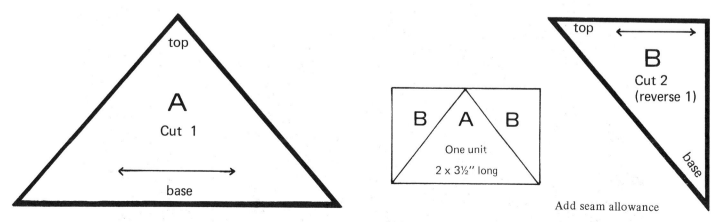

top

A

Cut 1

base

B   A   B

One unit

2 x 3½'' long

top

B

Cut 2
(reverse 1)

base

Add seam allowance

Plate 43. Two identical placemats of Hexagon Beauty, using the same fabrics illustrate the importance of fabric placement. By Gail Giberson.

Plate 42. The Jacob's Ladder pattern, assembled as yardage, was used for this man's sport shirt. Scraps from two color families are tied together by the repetition of navy blue in the large triangles. By Gail Giberson.

Plate 44. Four blocks of Bright Hopes set off by a red binding. By Joan Beucke.

Plate 45. The front of this needlework carrying bag is made from two blocks of a larger Hexagon Beauty. By Gail Giberson.

Plate 46. "Pine Tree" stands out more vividly when composed of contrasting fabrics. By Joan Beucke.

Plate 47. The Night and Noon design can give surprising results. The photo of four blocks on the left shows how many colors of scraps can be successfully combined by repeating one color consistently. By Joan Beucke. To the right is one block of Night and Noon done in a monochromatic color arrangement. By Mary Hobson.

Repeat of four blocks

12″ square

See Color Plate on Page 41

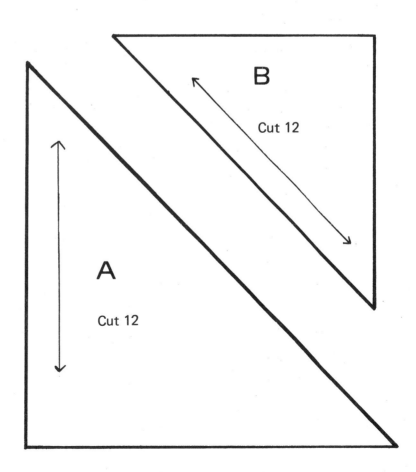

B

Cut 12

A

Cut 12

Add seam allowance

Bright Hopes

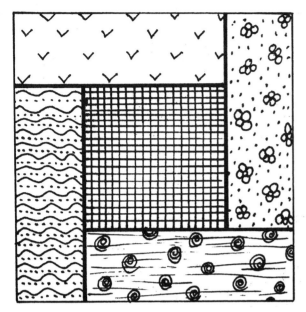

6" square
See Color Plate on Page 44

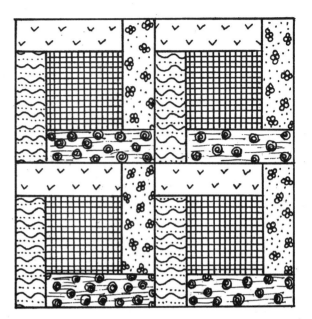

Repeat of four blocks

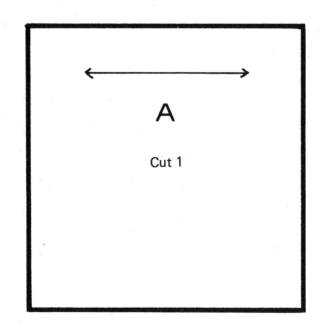

A

Cut 1

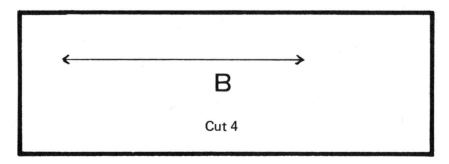

B

Cut 4

Add seam allowance

Star Of Many Points

Repeat of four blocks

14″ square
See Color Plate on Page 76

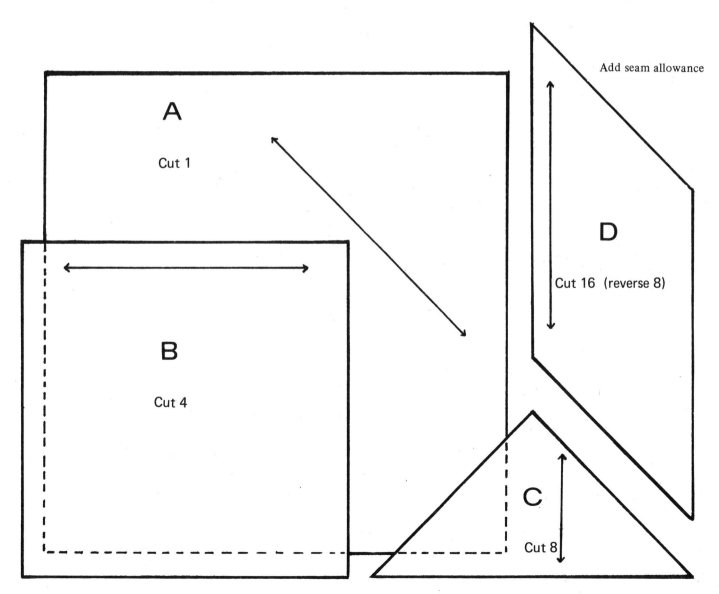

A
Cut 1

B
Cut 4

C
Cut 8

D
Cut 16 (reverse 8)

Add seam allowance

Pine Tree

10" square

See Color Plate on Page 44

Repeat of four blocks

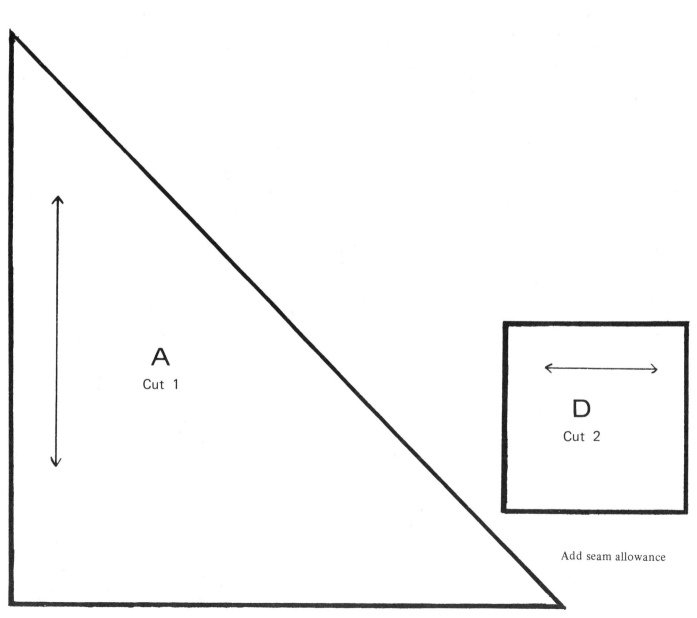

A

Cut 1

D

Cut 2

Add seam allowance

48

Repeat of eight blocks

Repeat of four blocks with bands

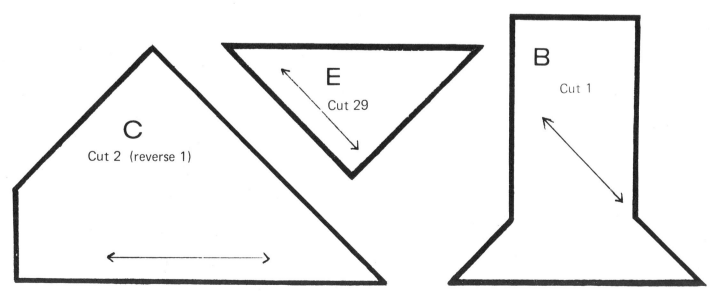

C
Cut 2 (reverse 1)

E
Cut 29

B
Cut 1

Mexican Star

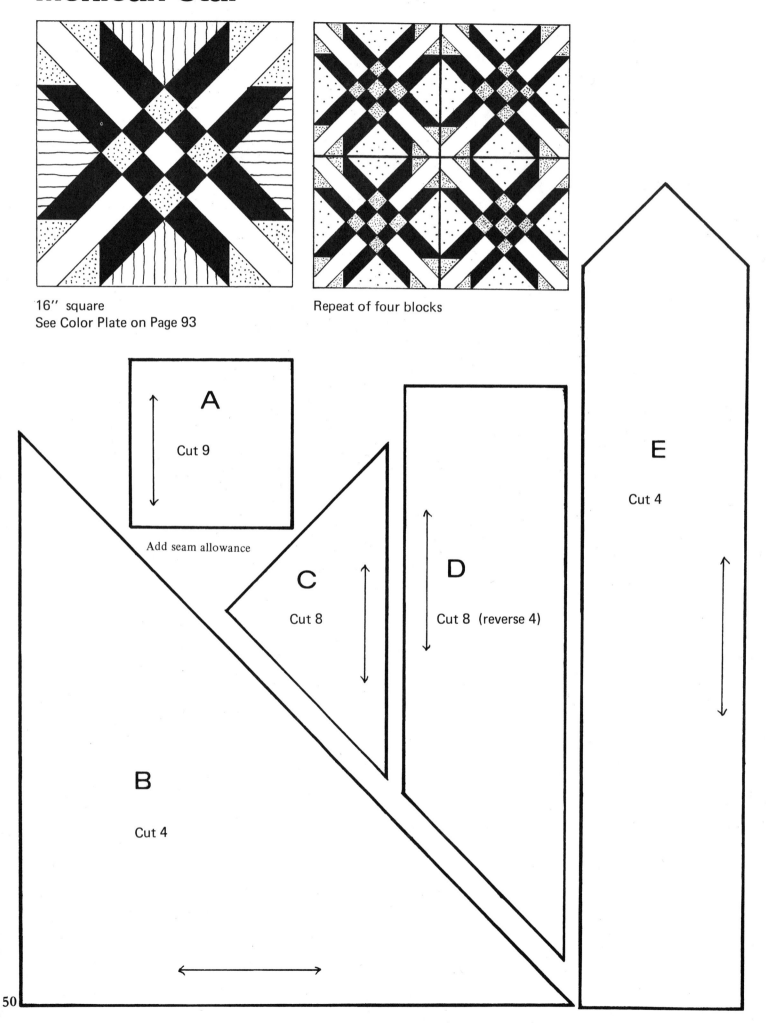

16'' square
See Color Plate on Page 93

Repeat of four blocks

A

Cut 9

Add seam allowance

B

Cut 4

C

Cut 8

D

Cut 8 (reverse 4)

E

Cut 4

Cross And Crown

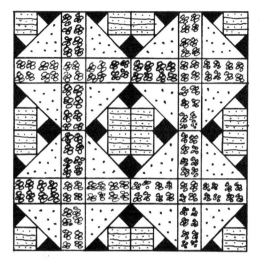

Repeat of four blocks
See Color Plate on Page 96

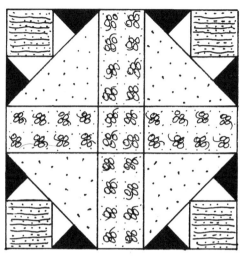

15" square

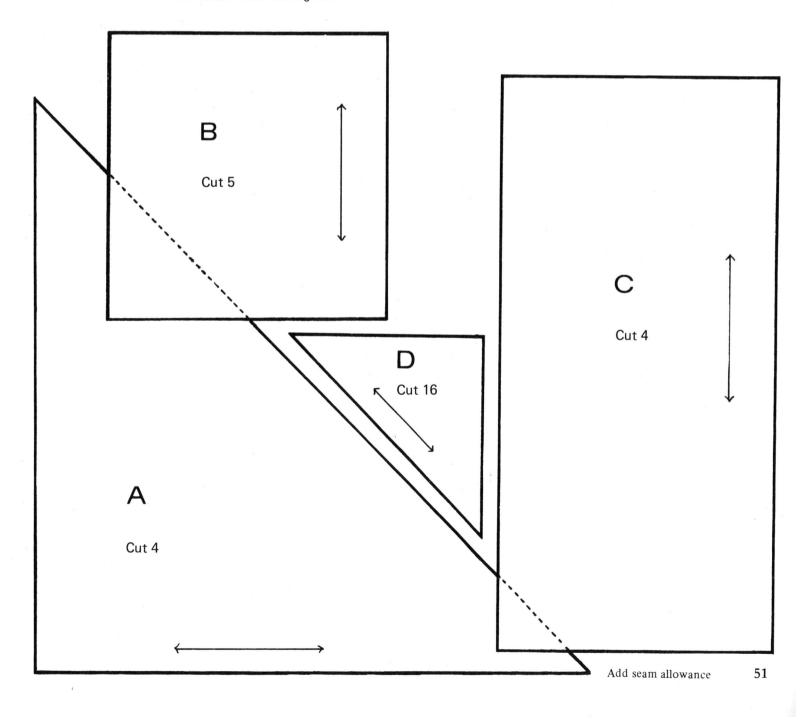

B
Cut 5

C
Cut 4

D
Cut 16

A
Cut 4

Add seam allowance   51

Missouri Puzzle

15″ square
See Color Plate on Page 93

Repeat of four blocks

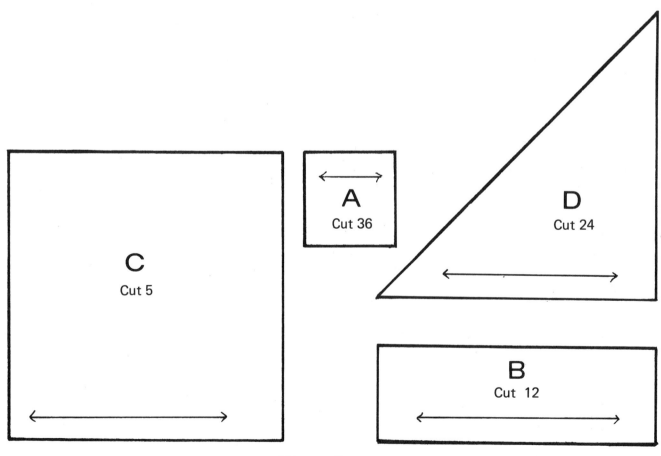

C
Cut 5

A
Cut 36

D
Cut 24

B
Cut 12

Add seam allowance

Machine Patchwork

The next ten patterns can easily be pieced by machine sewing from edge to edge. You will find that patchwork patterns which require setting a corner piece into an angle, ones with curved seams, or ones with tiny pieces are usually best done by hand until you have developed some experience sewing patchwork on the machine. Some people prefer doing all patchwork by hand, others prefer using the sewing machine, and some combine both methods. Give each method a try and then work the way that is best for you.

PREPARING TEMPLATES FOR MACHINE SEWING

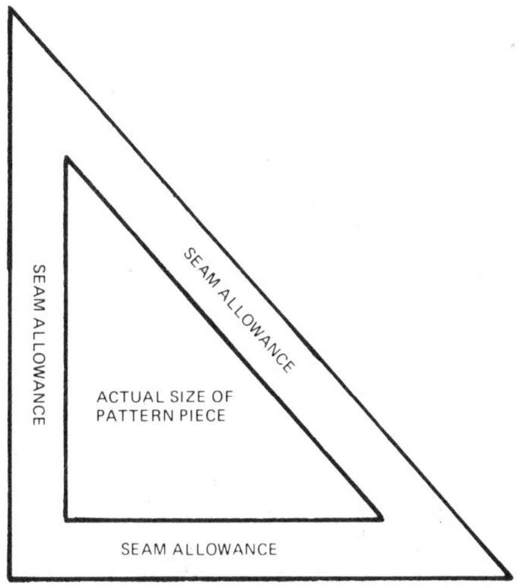

The template you prepare for cutting fabrics for machine patchwork must include the seam allowance. Prepare the templates for any pattern given in this section by tracing each shape and adding the seam allowance to all edges. (Fig. 1)

When adding the seam allowance, you can choose any width you like. While a ¼ inch seam allowance is used on most patchwork, we prefer to use a 3/8 inch seam allowance for machine work. The advantages of this are that it is easier to see the seam as it goes through the machine, especially with a wide presser foot; and it is easier to hold on to the fabric piece, keeping your fingers further away from the needle. Once you have chosen the seam allowance you like, use it for all seams on that pattern.

After you have added the seam allowances to all parts of the pattern, make sandpaper templates of each shape. Record on the back of each shape the name of the pattern to which it belongs, the amount of the seam allowance you have included and the line indicating the way the fabric grain should run. After you have cut the templates out of sandpaper and are ready to use them, check to be sure they are the right size. For instance, if you have a 3 inch square in your pattern and are using a 3/8 inch seam allowance, the template should measure 3¾ inch square. If it is a little off, fix it now as every error compounds itself in the final project.

MARKING AND CUTTING FABRICS

After preparing the templates, you will need to mark and cut the fabric. Accuracy here is important because the fabric edge is your sewing guide. There will be no pencil line to sew on as with pieces prepared for hand sewing. Be sure that the fabric you will be cutting is ironed smooth. Place the sandpaper side of your template on the wrong side of the material, matching the grain line. Mark around the edges of the template with your pencil. If you are marking many pieces from the same fabric, they can often be placed right next to each other and share a common line on one edge. (Fig. 2)

Fig. 1. Sandpaper template with seam allowance added for machine patchwork.

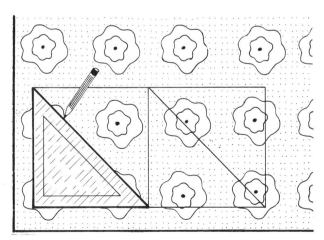

Fig. 2. Marking wrong side of fabric for machine patchwork.

With very sharp scissors, cut just to the inside of the edge of the marking line or right on the line if it is shared with another pattern piece.

If you are cutting many pieces of the same fabric and have very sharp scissors, you usually can cut through two thicknesses of fabric at the same time. Experiment with this to see if you can achieve smooth, accurate edges—it might save you some time.

CUTTING WITHOUT A TEMPLATE

Here is another method you might like to try for patterns that require a lot of the same size pieces (usually strips) like Rail Fence or Log Cabin. You can cut strips across the complete width of the material and then cut the strips off at the desired length.

Prepare a straight fabric edge across the width of your fabric. This can be done by pulling a thread across the fabric and trimming off the uneven edge. Another method is to fold the edge of the fabric back with the edges of the selvages even on both sides. Pull the fabric smooth and press a line with the iron. This will usually give you a straight line with which you can work. (Fig. 3)

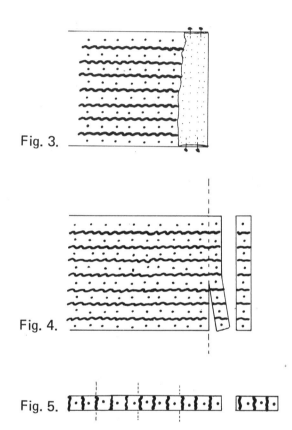

Fig. 3.

Fig. 4.

Fig. 5.

Once you have a straight edge to work with, determine the <u>width</u> of the strip you will need and add the amount of the seam allowance for <u>each side</u>. For example, if you need a lot of strips 1 inch wide for Rail Fence and are using a 3/8 inch seam allowance, you will need to cut the strips of fabric 1¾ inches wide. Measure over the 1¾ inches and mark the fabric. Continue to do this across the width of the fabric. Cut the fabric, using the marks as guides. (Fig. 4) Now you will have long strips of fabric that can be cut off at any <u>length</u> needed. If your fabric strip needs to be 4 inches long for your Rail Fence pattern, cut it off at 4¾ inches, and this will include your seam allowances at each end. (Fig. 5) This method works quite well for any pattern where you need to cut many strips or squares of one fabric.

JOINING THE FABRIC PIECES

Accuracy of the seam width is important, so it is essential that you have some type of a guide on your sewing machine for feeding the fabric to achieve the proper seam allowance. The throat plates on most sewing machines have guidelines marked. If your machine has these, be sure they are accurate and that there is a mark for the seam width you are using. If there isn't a guideline, you can make one with masking tape. To do this, lower your needle into the machine, measure out from the needle the distance of the seam allowance and place the edge of the masking tape there.

When you are ready to sew two pieces of fabric together, place them with right sides together and pin them in one or two places, being sure that the edges are even. (Fig. 6) Basting is not necessary. Feed the piece through your machine right along the guideline and stitch from edge to edge. Backstitching is not necessary because the seams will be locked when crossed by another patch in the block.

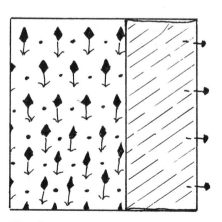

Fig. 6.

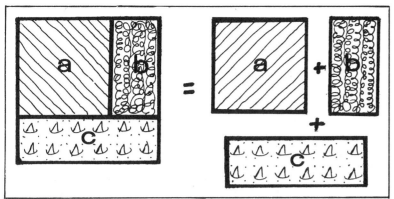

Fig. 7

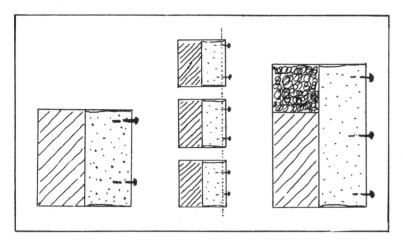

Fig. 8

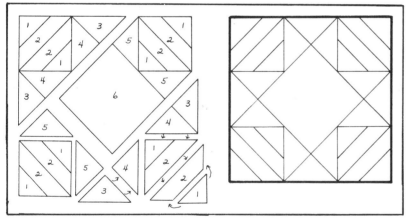

Fig. 9

If you have to join a large number of pieces for a quilt or similar project, you should try to build all the blocks in the project at the same time in an assembly-line fashion. This is much faster than piecing one block at a time.

To do this, cut all the pieces for the project at once. As an example, say you need twelve blocks of the one in Fig. 7. Cut twelve pieces each of A, B and C.

Pin piece A to B for all twelve blocks and feed them through the sewing machine in a continuous string. (Fig. 8) As you reach the end of the stitching on one piece, set the next piece at the beginning of the feed dog on the sewing machine and it will feed it right through, leaving a few threads between the pieces. Snip the threads between them and then join piece C to all twelve blocks in the same manner. This will speed up the tedious process of joining many small pieces together.

PIECING THE BLOCK

You will need to analyze your pattern to decide how to go about putting it together from its smallest units to the large block and take advantage of sewing from edge to edge. Try to visualize the block taken apart in units and ask yourself some questions. Are there lines that divide the entire block (go from one edge to the other)? Are there lines that divide that section further? Keep dissecting each section until you come to the smallest unit. That is where you will start to build the block together. The example in Fig. 9 will help you visualize this.

Dotted lines on the pattern diagrams in this section indicate the major divisions of the block. If you are having to set a piece into an angle or otherwise are having difficulty, analyze your pattern again.

When joining the sections of the pattern together, be sure to match the seams. You may need to stretch or ease some pieces slightly to make the seams meet exactly.

JOINING BLOCKS FOR A LARGER PROJECT

After you have pieced a number of blocks of the same pattern and want to join them together for a large project, it is best to check the blocks and "square them up" before joining them. For instance, if you are working with an 8 inch block and are using 3/8 inch seams, your blocks should be 8¾ inches square. Try to fix any that aren't quite right by trimming them a little if they are too large. If one edge is a little small, try to compensate for this when joining the blocks.

Usually you can join the blocks together in horizontal rows and then join the rows together to make up the larger project. When joining the rows, be sure that the seam lines of the blocks match up exactly. If you pin at each point where the seam lines meet, you can sometimes ease or stretch the fabric between to make the blocks match. If they don't, take a few seams apart and do some repair.

Night And Noon

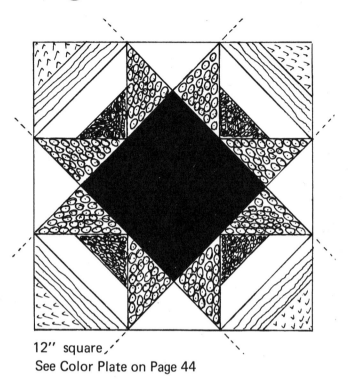

12″ square
See Color Plate on Page 44

Repeat of four blocks

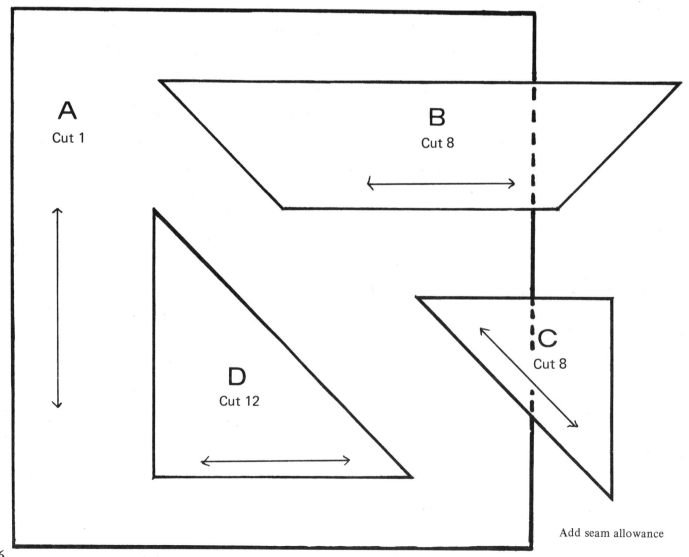

A
Cut 1

B
Cut 8

C
Cut 8

D
Cut 12

Add seam allowance

56

Framed Square

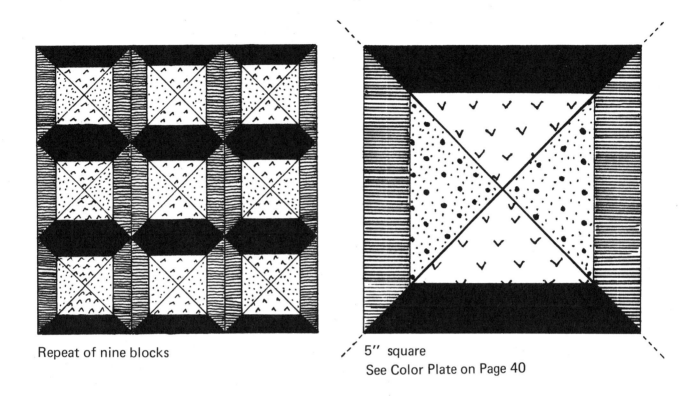

Repeat of nine blocks

5" square
See Color Plate on Page 40

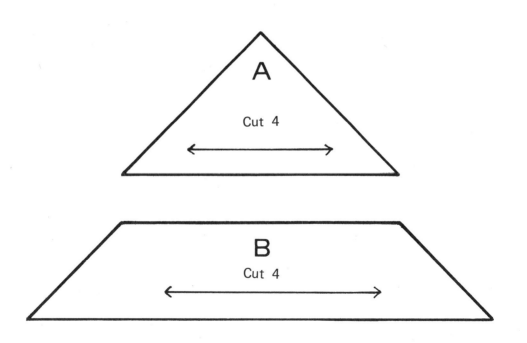

A
Cut 4

B
Cut 4

Add seam allowance

Patience Corner

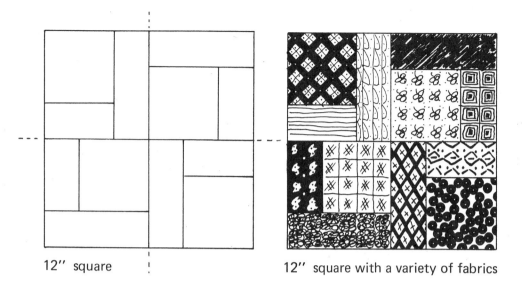

12" square

12" square with a variety of fabrics

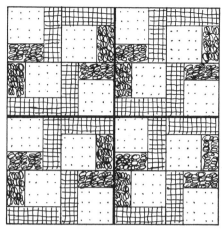

Repeat of four blocks
See Color Plate on Page 41

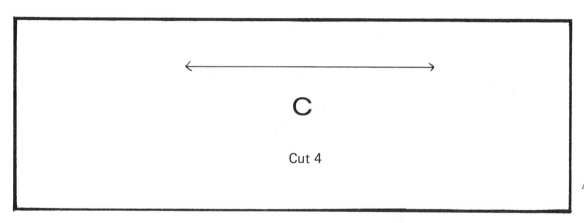

C

Cut 4

Add seam allowance

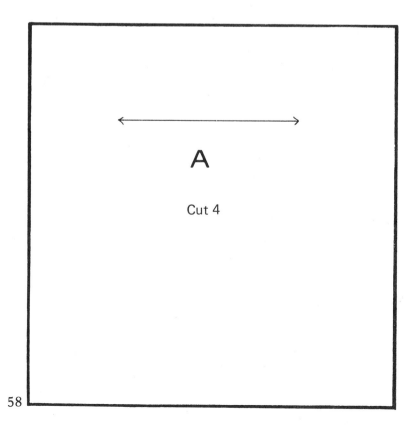

A

Cut 4

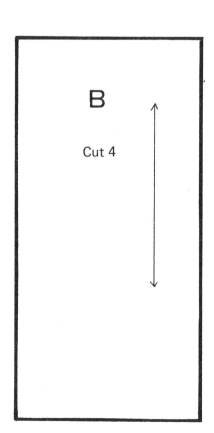

B

Cut 4

House On A Hill

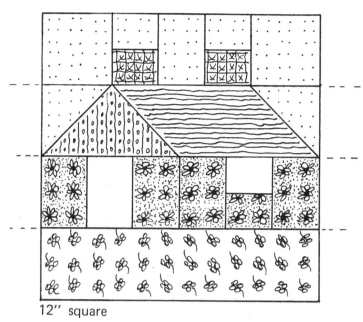

12" square

See Color Plate on Front Cover

Add seam allowance

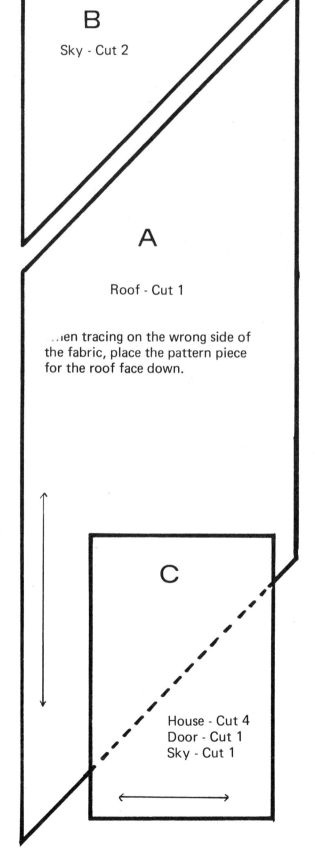

B

Sky - Cut 2

A

Roof - Cut 1

...en tracing on the wrong side of the fabric, place the pattern piece for the roof face down.

C

House - Cut 4
Door - Cut 1
Sky - Cut 1

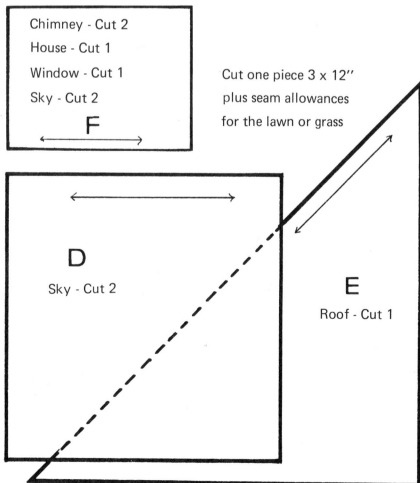

Chimney - Cut 2
House - Cut 1
Window - Cut 1
Sky - Cut 2

F

Cut one piece 3 x 12"
plus seam allowances
for the lawn or grass

D

Sky - Cut 2

E

Roof - Cut 1

Bear's Paw

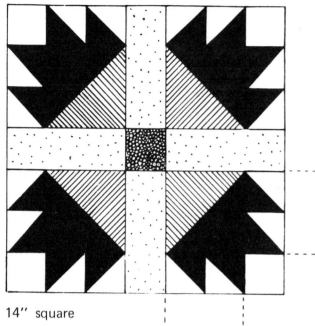

14" square

See Color Plate on Page 73

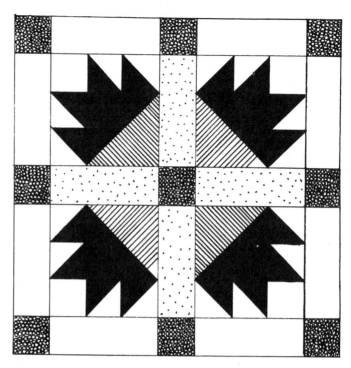

18" square (14" unit with outside bands added)

Other common names for this pattern are: Duck's Foot In The Mud, Bear's Foot, Goose Tracks and Hand of Friendship.

Four variations, all using the same pattern pieces, are given to show how fabric placement and selection can alter a design's appearance.

To add bands to the basic block as shown in the top right illustration, cut an additional 8 pieces of pattern D and 8 pieces of pattern C.

Variations 1 and 2 use pattern A as a square shape. The saw-toothed edge was achieved by cutting 16 of pattern B from the same fabric as pattern A.

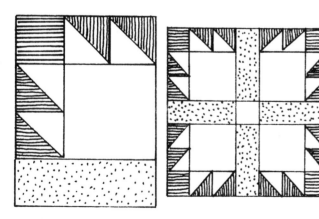

Variation 1

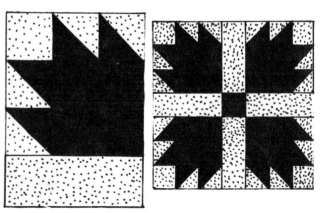

Variation 2

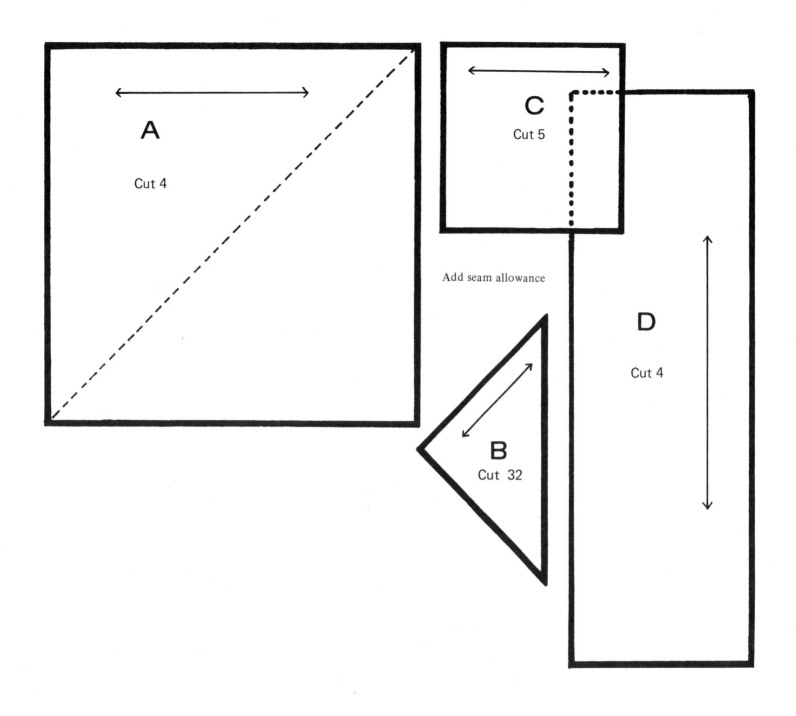

A

Cut 4

C

Cut 5

Add seam allowance

D

Cut 4

B

Cut 32

Variations 3 and 4 use the triangle made by cutting pattern A along the dotted line.

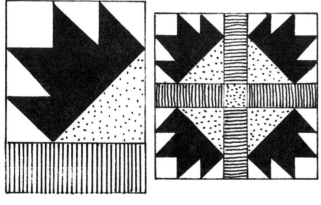

Variation 3

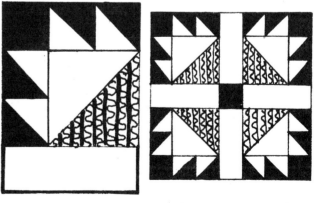

Variation 4

Log Cabin

CONSIDER DESIGN AND COLOR VARIATIONS

Log Cabin is one of the oldest types of patchwork. It consists of pieced blocks in which light and dark strips of fabric are sewn together, building out from a center square. Usually the strips are arranged so that when the block is divided on the diagonal, half is light and half is dark. (Fig. 1)

There are many other ways that the colors can be arranged in a Log Cabin block to produce some interesting variations. (Fig. 2 through 4 and Color Plate 39 & 40) Notice how two fabrics were used to make an interesting spiral effect in Color Plate 40.

If you make a large project such as a wall hanging or quilt out of the standard block shown in Fig. 1, the blocks can be arranged into one of many patterns, and a definite design will emerge. The design below illustrates a few of the many ways the blocks can be arranged.

Two color families could be used in place of the light/dark contrasts for very striking effects. (Color Plates 50 & 54, and Cover) Log Cabin can also be a good design for using up scraps when you divide them into light and dark groups. You may experience some difficulty deciding if some fabrics will read light or dark in the finished block. The wall hanging in Color Plate 53 illustrates this.

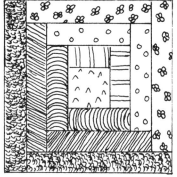

Fig. 1

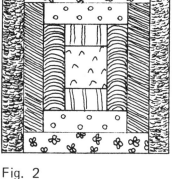

Fig. 2

Fig. 3

Fig. 4

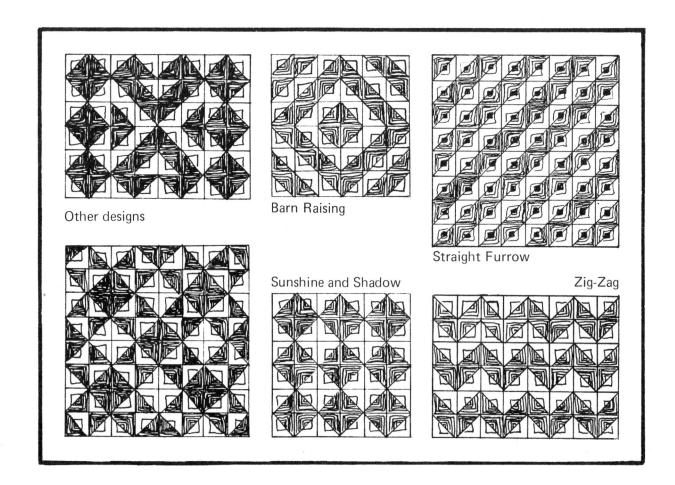

Other designs

Barn Raising

Straight Furrow

Sunshine and Shadow

Zig-Zag

SUITABLE FABRICS

Broadcloth-weight cotton or cotton blends will adapt best to this design for a quilt or large project. This weight of fabric will be easy to quilt and is light enough not to make a large project too heavy. Double knit polyesters would be fine, especially in pillows or floor cushions; however, these would probably not be quilted due to their thickness.

In the past, velvets, silks, woolens, etc. were used in Log Cabin designs. The pattern pieces were cut out in the same manner as the ones we will cut, but they were sewn to a foundation block in a crazy patchwork method to help give them body and keep them from stretching and slipping.

MAKING TEMPLATES AND CUTTING FABRICS

Enlarge the diagram in Fig. 5 to make full size templates. This can be easily accomplished by using graph paper. Draw an 8 inch square on the graph paper and draw strips 1 inch wide in the same design as the figure. The result will be an 8 inch block consisting of twelve strips 1 inch wide and a 2 inch center square. Larger blocks can be made by adding more strips to the outside of the diagram in the same sequence.

By studying the diagram, you will see that most of the sizes are repeated. Therefore, you will need to make templates for only the following strips: 1, 2, 3 5, 7, 9, 11 and 13. When making the templates, be sure to add a seam allowance to all of the edges.

You could also cut the strips for Log Cabin in the manner discussed in the Machine Patchwork section on cutting fabrics without a template, Page 54.

Decide which fabrics will be used for each strip, keeping in mind your color arrangement. In the standard Log Cabin arrangement, as in Fig. 1 and the illustrations to the left, the fabrics should be arranged so that the lightest shades are toward the center. Determine which size template (s) you will use for each fabric and record that on a list or write it on the master pattern. Cut the number of pieces you will need to complete the project.

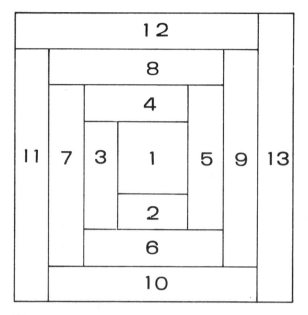

Fig. 5

ASSEMBLING SEQUENCE

In Fig. 5 the strips are numbered in a clockwise manner from the center square out, showing the order in which they are joined together. Place the pieces right sides together, and join them until the entire block is pieced. When all of the blocks have been pieced, experiment with them to get the arrangement of light and dark that pleases you.

QUILTING

The most popular quilting pattern for Log Cabin is to quilt parallel to and just inside the seam lines of the pieces. The design of Log Cabin is so busy that an elaborate quilting design would be lost. If you use heavy fabrics or don't wish to quilt each block, tying or tufting would be sufficient.

FINISHING

The light/dark contrasts of Log Cabin and the designs that emerge from the various arrangements show up best in large projects such as quilts and wall hangings. Individual blocks of Log Cabin are effective as pillows, seat cushions, pockets and placemats. Decorative borders are not usually used on Log Cabin quilts.

King's X

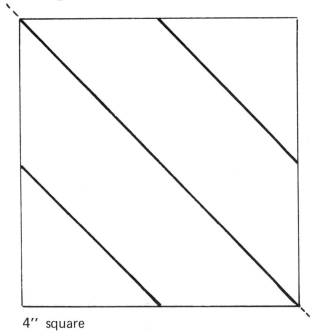

4″ square

See Color Plate on Page 69

Repeat of 16 blocks in two fabrics

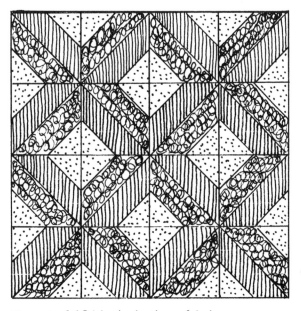

Repeat of 16 blocks in three fabrics

Repeat of 16 blocks in four fabrics

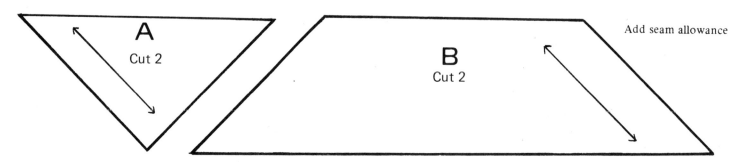

A
Cut 2

B
Cut 2

Add seam allowance

Repeat of nine blocks

One block

See Color Plates on Pages 37 & 97

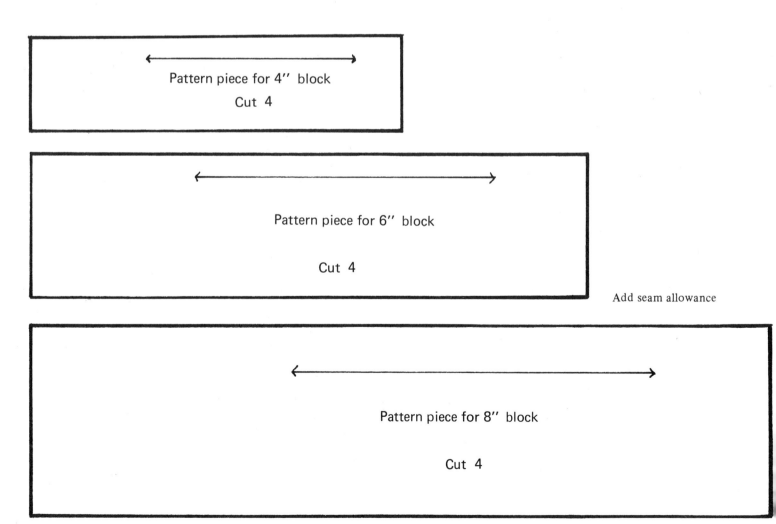

Pattern piece for 4" block

Cut 4

Pattern piece for 6" block

Cut 4

Add seam allowance

Pattern piece for 8" block

Cut 4

Hexagon Beauty

CONSIDER DESIGN AND COLOR VARIATIONS

Hexagon Beauty consists of six triangles which fit together to form a large hexagon. (Fig. 1) Each triangle is made of two pieces (A and B) which give the pattern further design possibilities. Another pattern piece (C) can be added to square off the corners or provide a straight edge on a quilt; however adding piece C will <u>not</u> give you a square block, but rather a rectangle. (Fig. 2)

Usually the hexagons are assembled in a honeycomb fashion. (Fig. 3) A variation called Whirling Triangles is shown in Fig. 4. When designing this one, various fabrics may be used for pattern piece B, even a different one for each block. One plain fabric, preferably dark, should be used throughout the design for pattern piece A. This will highlight the pinwheel effect.

Choosing fabrics for Hexagon Beauty can be somewhat tricky. First, you should consider what part of the design you want to highlight. As you will notice in Color Plate 43, when darker or more intense fabrics are used for pattern piece B, the hexagon shape will show up better. Dark fabrics on the alternating inside triangles could make the finished article look like you are advertising a fallout shelter. Both placemats in Color Plate 43 used the same four fabrics, so you can see the definite variation you get when you change the fabric placements.

MAKING TEMPLATES AND CUTTING FABRIC

This pattern is very suitable for machine sewing. Trace the pattern pieces and add seam allowances to all sides of each piece as explained in the discussion of machine patchwork. Following the grain lines, cut six each of pattern pieces A and B for each hexagon shape. If you use pattern piece C, be sure to reverse half of the templates on your fabric so they will be facing the right direction in the finished article.

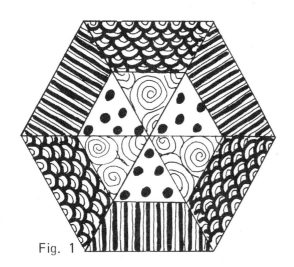

Fig. 1

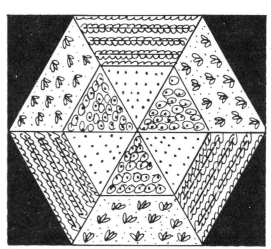

Fig. 2

Fig. 3

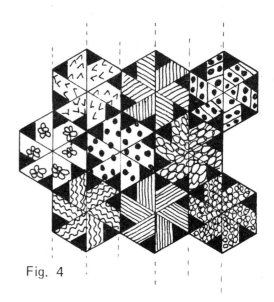

Fig. 4

ASSEMBLING SEQUENCE OF BLOCK

To assemble one block of Hexagon Beauty, begin by joining piece A to piece B for all six triangles. Join the triangles together in two groups of three each, then put the two groups together. (Fig. 5 & 6).

If you are going to join more than one hexagon together for a large project, don't construct the hexagons first and then try to fit them together. An easier approach is to analyze the project and piece it row by row horizontally. The hexagons will take shape as the rows are pieced. The dotted lines in Fig. 3 show how a large project is divided into horizontal rows.

QUILTING

Outline quilting is probably the most suitable for this design. In Color Plate 43, you will notice that the placemat with the green circles is quilted just outside and inside the green rings. This tends to make the rings and the hexagon shape stand out more. The other placemat is quilted more heavily.

FINISHING

The placemats in the color plate are made of thirty-two triangles (which make up four hexagons) and the fill-in triangles. If you use pattern pieces A and B provided here and piece the placemats according to Fig. 7, you will have a finished placemat that measures about 14 x 20 inches. Backing fabric was brought around to finish the edges.

When using the Hexagon Beauty or Whirling Triangles design for a quilt or large project, the hexagons can be fit together in a honeycomb fashion, and pattern piece C can be used to make a straight edge. (Fig. 3) An alternate method would be to allow the hexagons, themselves, to make a nice scalloped border.

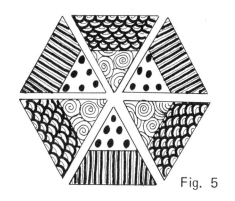

Fig. 5

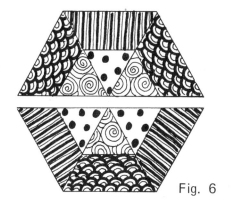

Fig. 6

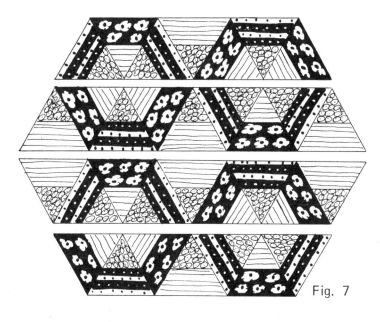

Fig. 7

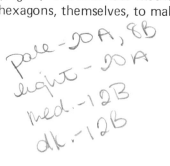

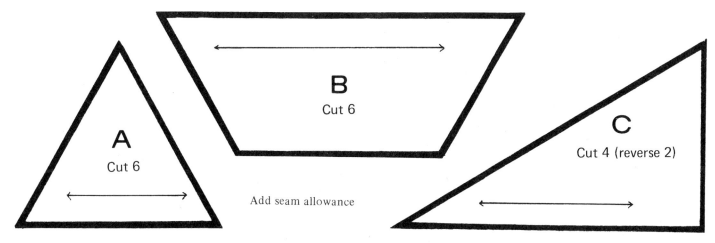

A
Cut 6

B
Cut 6

C
Cut 4 (reverse 2)

Add seam allowance

Jacob's Ladder

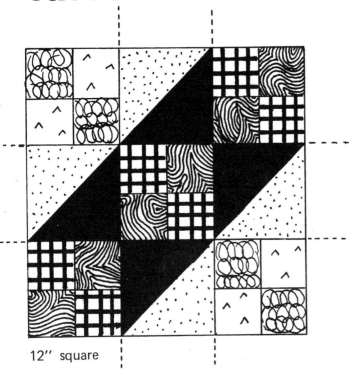

12" square

See Color Plates on Pages 44 & 72

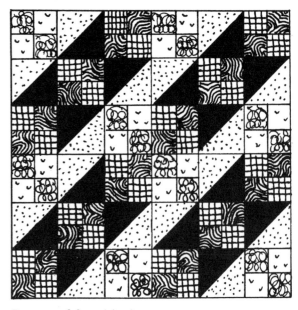

Repeat of four blocks

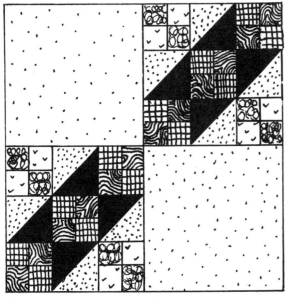

Two blocks with two plain squares

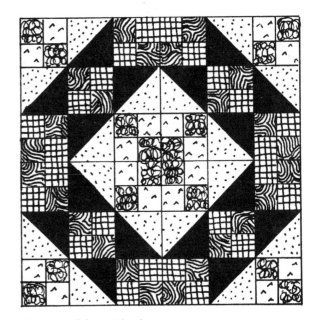

Repeat of four blocks

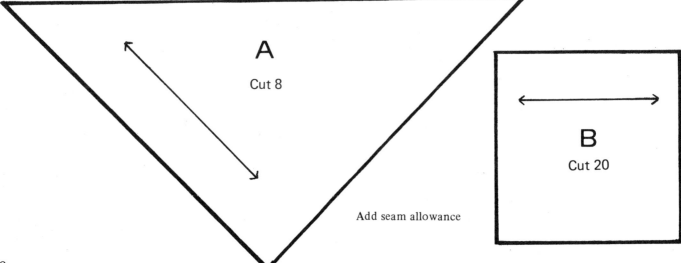

A

Cut 8

B

Cut 20

Add seam allowance

Plate 48. This King's X skirt was designed by repeating three fabrics. By Donna Swenson.

Plate 49. Four blocks of Potted Star Flower form a stunning center of this wall hanging. Clamshells and Spools form the top and bottom borders. By Melinda Santa Cruz.

Plate 50. Two color families, separated on the diagonal, were used in this Log Cabin pillow. By Marjorie Puckett.

Plate 51. A fabric covered with appliqued clamshells was attached to the front of this straw handbag. By Debby Ferguson. The vibrant Lemon Star design was by Myrna Schatzman.

Plate 52. The beauty of patchwork lends itself to many items from sleeves on dresses, hatbands, borders in skirts, to placemats, chair cushions, wall hangings, table runners and other numerous items.

69

Eight Piece Centers

The following section has eight different traditional patterns or blocks in it, all containing eight piece centers. The beginning patchwork student should have immediate success and perfect results if she uses our suggested procedure. Even if the reader is an experienced patchworker, she will quickly see its advantages: The patchwork will always lay flat and smooth where the eight patches meet. Try the same techniques described when piecing six piece centers.

PINNING

Lay the eight pieces to be assembled out in front of you in the pattern they will form. Take two pieces lying next to each other and pin them, right sides together. Check to see that the pins, inserted at the pencil corners, emerge on the back side also at the pencil corners. Insert pins along the pencil line as often as needed, usually about 1½ inches apart. The traditional patterns in this section will require only two or three pins.

SEWING

For right-handed people, sew from right to left. Begin your hand stitch where the pin is inserted at the corners. Sew halfway across on the pencil line, using the recommended hand stitch for patchwork. (P. 14) Sew the remaining half of the seam in the usual manner, but take a slightly deeper seam allowance, or stitch in or below the pencil line by about 1/16 inch. <u>Be sure that you take the deeper seam only on the last half of it, working toward the tip or point where all eight pieces eventually meet.</u> Sew only to the pin that is inserted at the pencil corners. Fasten off your thread, and trim off the point across the ends of the fabric. This is to remove the excess fabric, but don't trim too close to where your stitching ends.

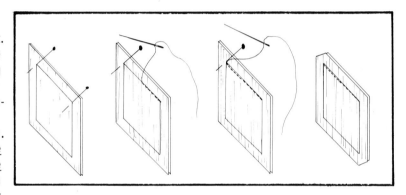

SEQUENCE

Plan to assemble your eight patches into quarters, then halves. As you sew, finger press the seams to one side, and have all the seams going in the same direction, clockwise or counter-clockwise.

To sew the two halves together, join them with their right sides together and match them at their centers. Pin the halves at both ends at their pencil corners. Check carefully to see that your pins emerge on the back side at the pencil corners just as on the front. Start sewing, working toward the center, and begin your deeper seam one-half of the way across. When you get to the center where the eight pieces meet, lift the seam allowances away so they are not stitched down. Continue stitching across, returning to your pencil line three-quarters of the way across.

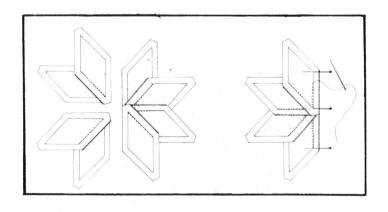

Stars And Cubes

  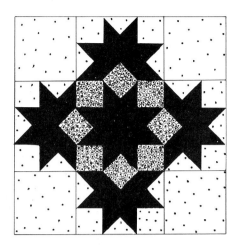

18" square (showing different fabric placements)
See Color Plate on Page 93

 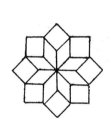 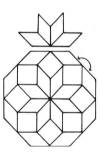  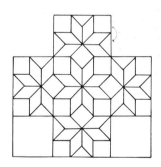

Suggested sequence for assembling Stars and Cubes

Cut 4 corner pieces, 5 3/8" square, plus seam allowances

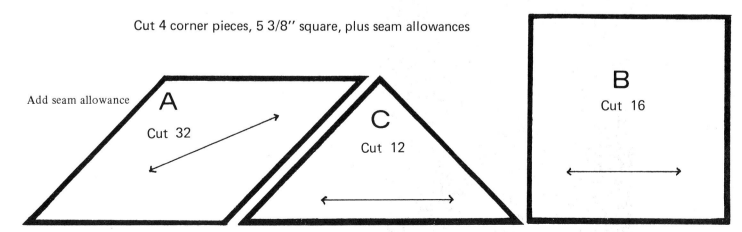

Add seam allowance

A
Cut 32

C
Cut 12

B
Cut 16

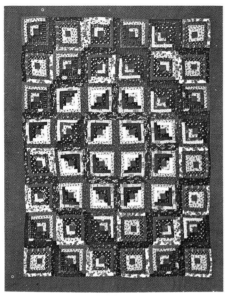

Plate 53. These forty-eight blocks of Log Cabin have been arranged in the stunning Barn Raising Design. Wall hanging by Mary Hobson.

Plate 54. This striking wall hanging consists of sixteen blocks assembled in the Sunshine and Shadow variation of Log Cabin. By Melodie Turnham.

Plate 55. This variation of Drunkard's Path is usually best when done in two contrasting fabrics. By Dorothy Denton.

Plate 56. By utilizing the outline of the spools, additional interest is added to a project. By Marjorie Puckett.

Plate 57. Patchwork lends itself to many moods. Placemats by Gail Giberson.

Plate 58. Jacob's Ladder adapts well to larger projects because it can be quickly and accurately assembled on the machine. Table throw by Marjorie Puckett.

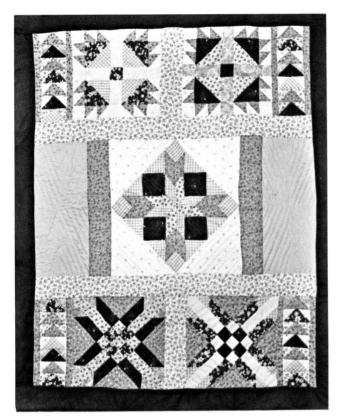

Plate 59. Wall hanging by Janelle Kennedy.

The Bear's Paw can be interpreted in a variety of pattern shapes and fabrics. The tote bag in Plate 60 shows an arrangement in two fabrics, while below it in Plate 61 three fabrics have been combined. The two Bear's Paw designs bordering the wall hanging in Plate 59 used four fabrics each and show the potential of this design through selection of color. Also shown in the wall hanging are Love-In-A-Mist, Mexican Star and Goose Tracks.

Plate 60. Totebag by Valerie Rudaitis.

Plate 61. Block executed by Joan Beucke.

Plate 62. Glorified Nine Patch in four combined units. By Lila More.

Plate 63. Four blocks of Robbing Peter to Pay Paul. This design gets its name from the reversal of colors in alternating blocks. By Joan Beucke.

Plate 64. One block of the Jinx Star pattern. By Lila More.

Love-In-A-Mist

10½″ square
See Color Plate on Page 40

Repeat of four blocks

Repeat of four blocks

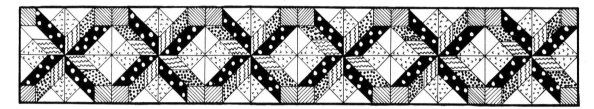

Repeat of six blocks

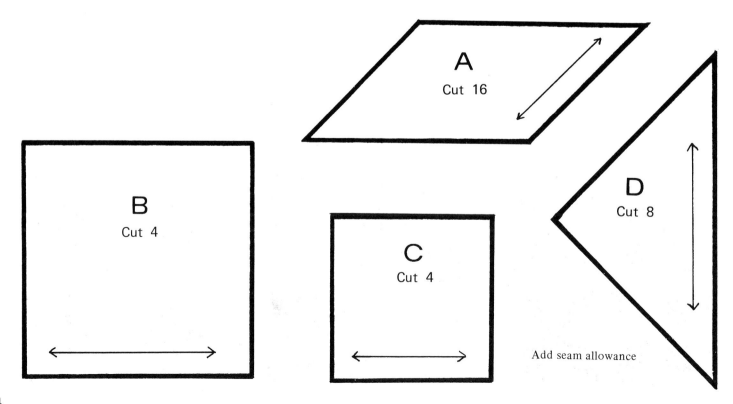

A
Cut 16

B
Cut 4

C
Cut 4

D
Cut 8

Add seam allowance

Lemon Star

Repeat of four blocks

15" square

See Color Plates on Pages 69 & 97

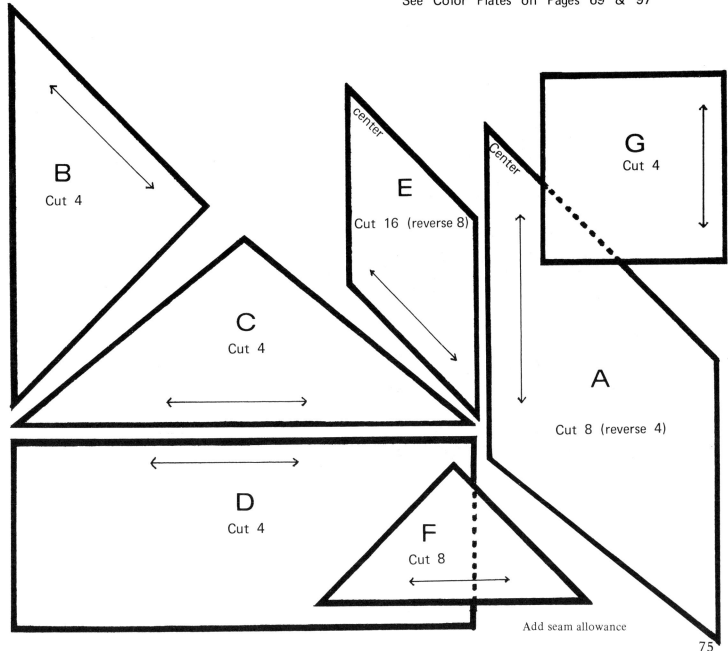

B
Cut 4

C
Cut 4

center

E
Cut 16 (reverse 8)

D
Cut 4

F
Cut 8

Center

G
Cut 4

A
Cut 8 (reverse 4)

Add seam allowance

Plate 65. Three fabrics have been beautifully combined in this Drunkard's Path. By Kathy Haas.

Plate 66. Four different green fabrics give richness to this Morning Star. By Louellen Sweinhart.

Plate 67. This Star of Many Points, in three fabrics, uses the darker color to define the points of the star. By Donna Swenson.

Plate 68. The Clamshell gives this child's dress a delicate trim. By Carolyn Felix.

Plate 69. Nautical theme pillows accent this boy's room.

14″ octagon

Repeat of four blocks

Morning Star

14″ square

See Color Plates on Pages 76 & 100

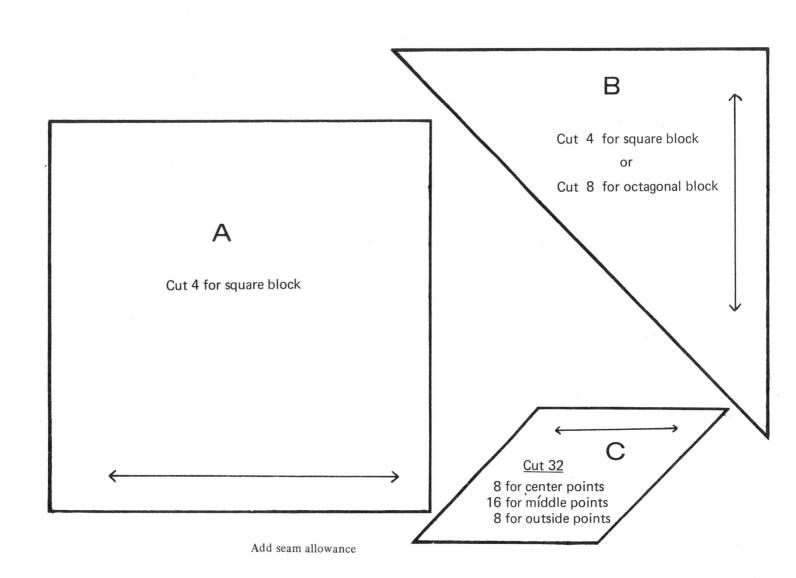

B

Cut 4 for square block

or

Cut 8 for octagonal block

A

Cut 4 for square block

C

Cut 32

8 for center points
16 for middle points
8 for outside points

Add seam allowance

Squared Star

14'' square
See Color Plate on Page 96

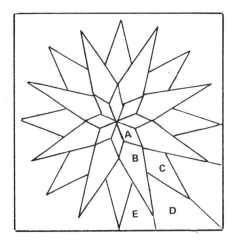

Repeat of four blocks

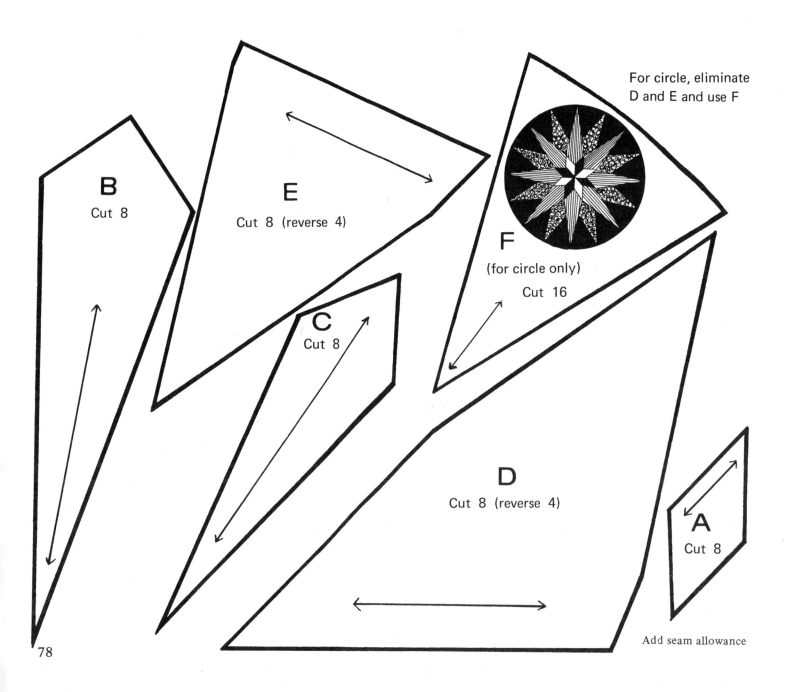

For circle, eliminate
D and E and use F

B
Cut 8

E
Cut 8 (reverse 4)

C
Cut 8

F
(for circle only)
Cut 16

D
Cut 8 (reverse 4)

A
Cut 8

Add seam allowance

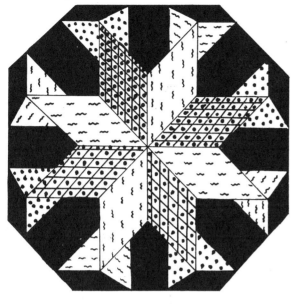

14" circle

Repeat of four circles
See Color Plate on Page 93

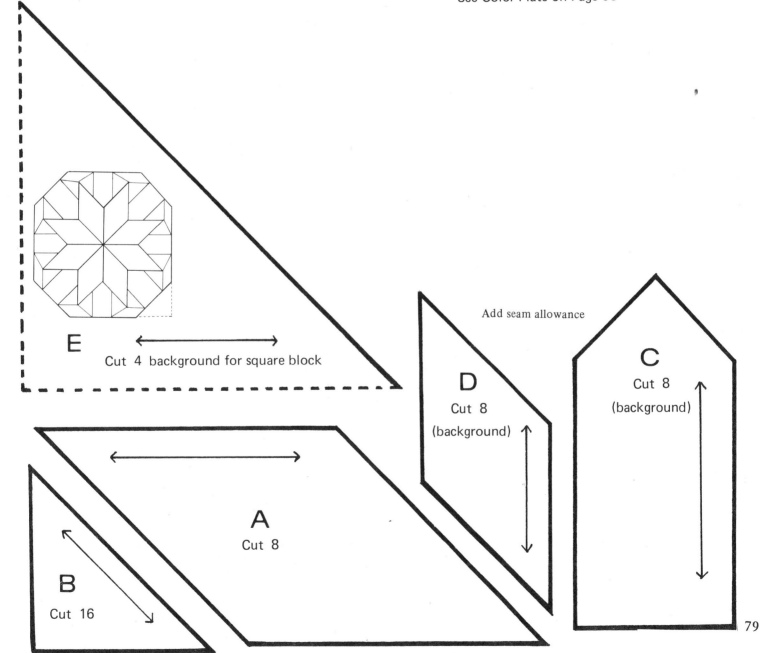

E

Cut 4 background for square block

Add seam allowance

D
Cut 8
(background)

C
Cut 8
(background)

A
Cut 8

B
Cut 16

Potted Star Flower

15½'' square

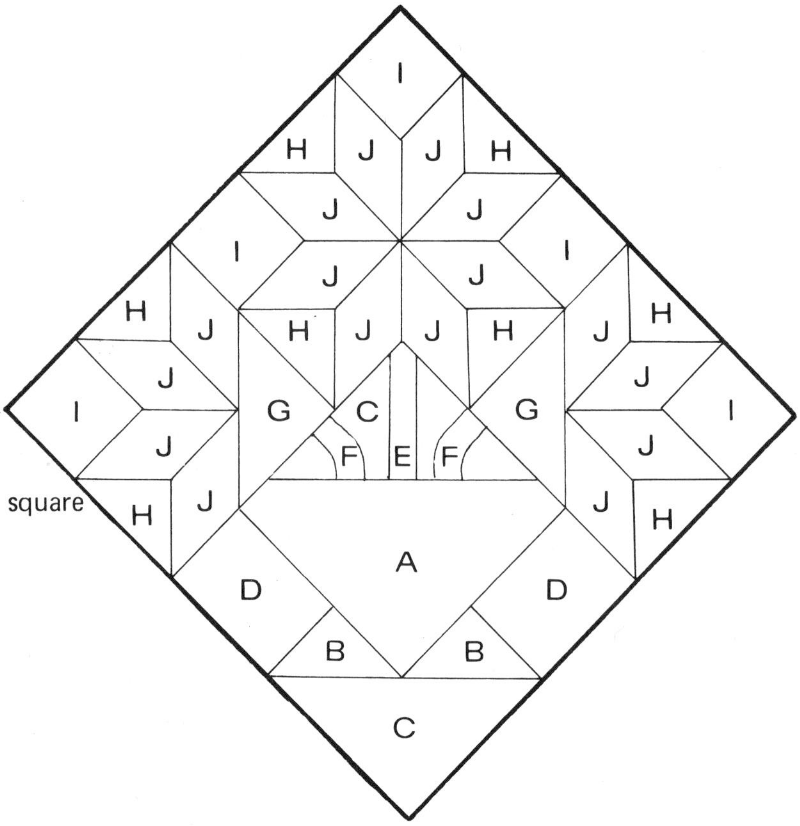

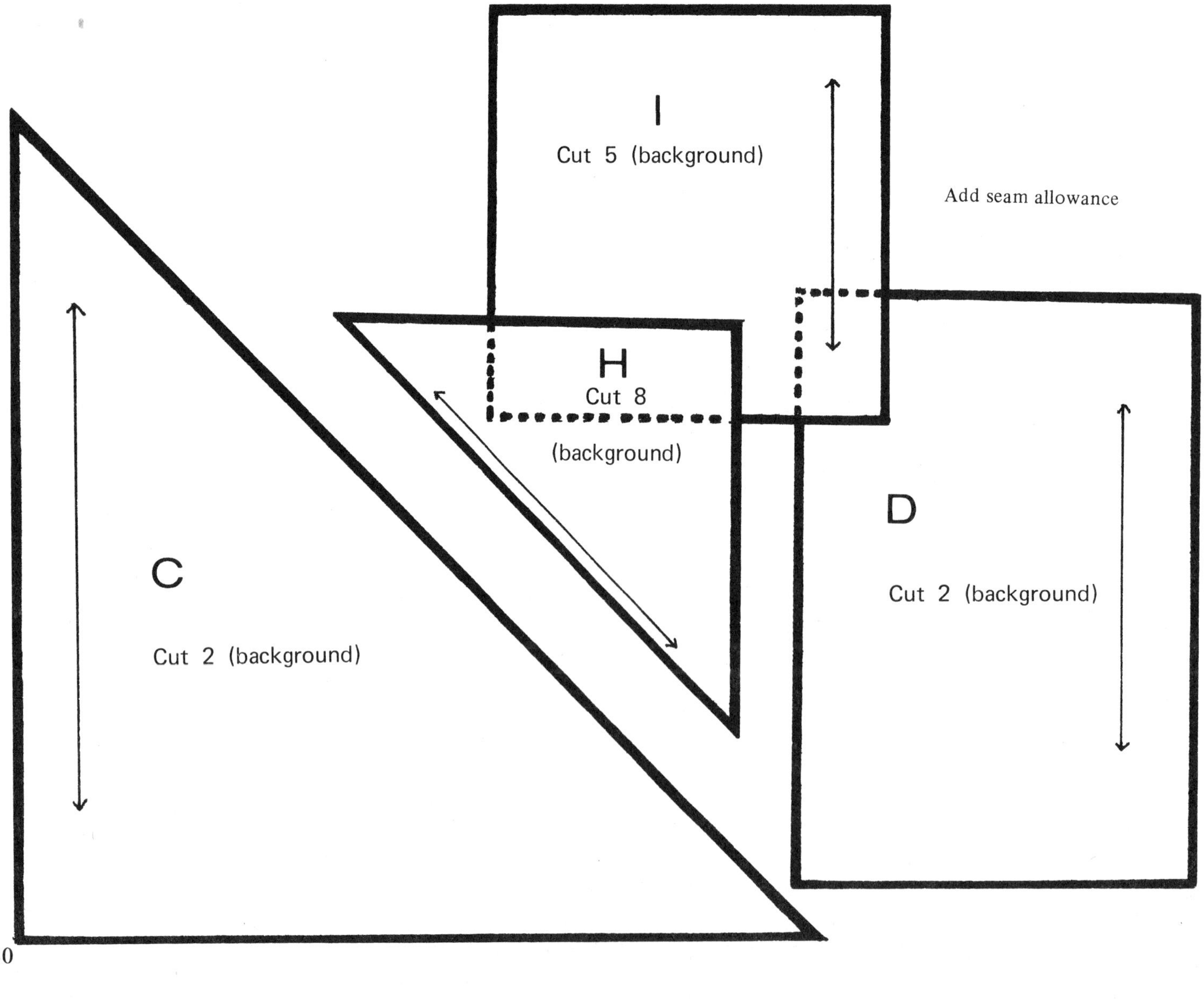

Block diagram with labeled pieces:
I / H J J H / J J / I J J I / H J H J H J H / J J / I G C F E F G I / J J / H J H J H J H / D A D / B B / C

I
Cut 5 (background)

Add seam allowance

H
Cut 8
(background)

C
Cut 2 (background)

D
Cut 2 (background)

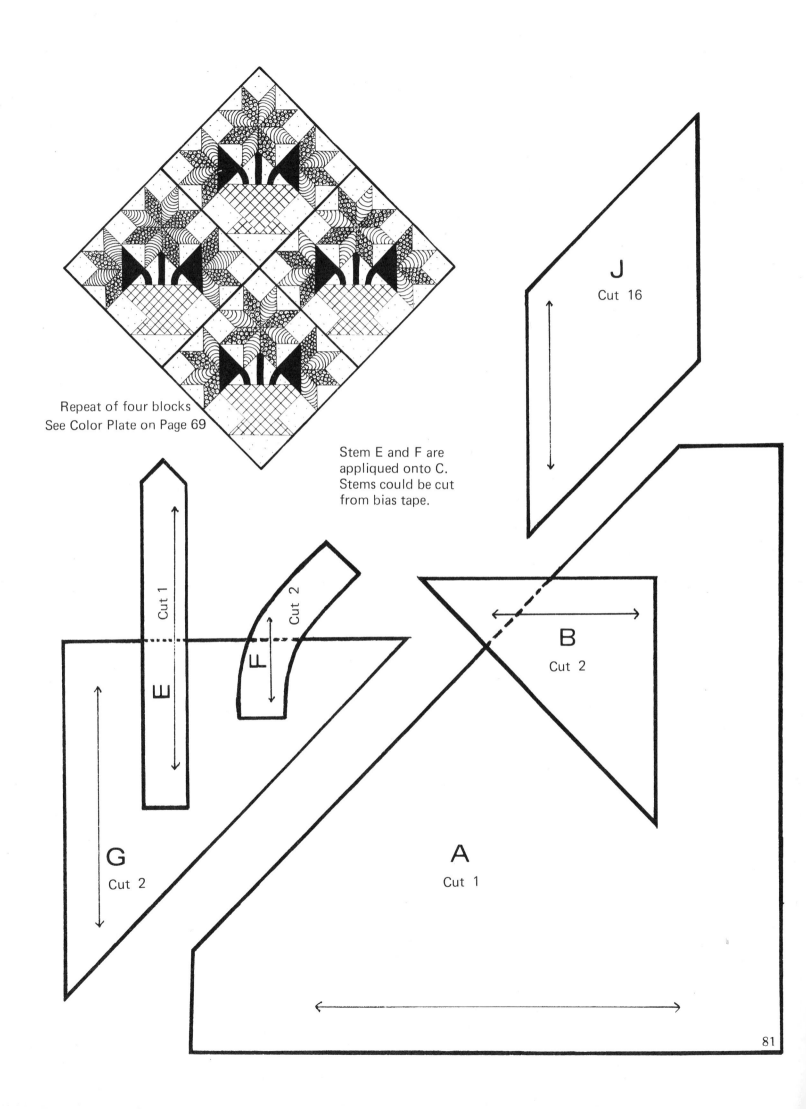

Repeat of four blocks
See Color Plate on Page 69

Stem E and F are
appliqued onto C.
Stems could be cut
from bias tape.

J
Cut 16

E
Cut 1

F
Cut 2

B
Cut 2

G
Cut 2

A
Cut 1

Christmas Star

16½" square
See Color Plate on Page 93

Yardage of continuous blocks

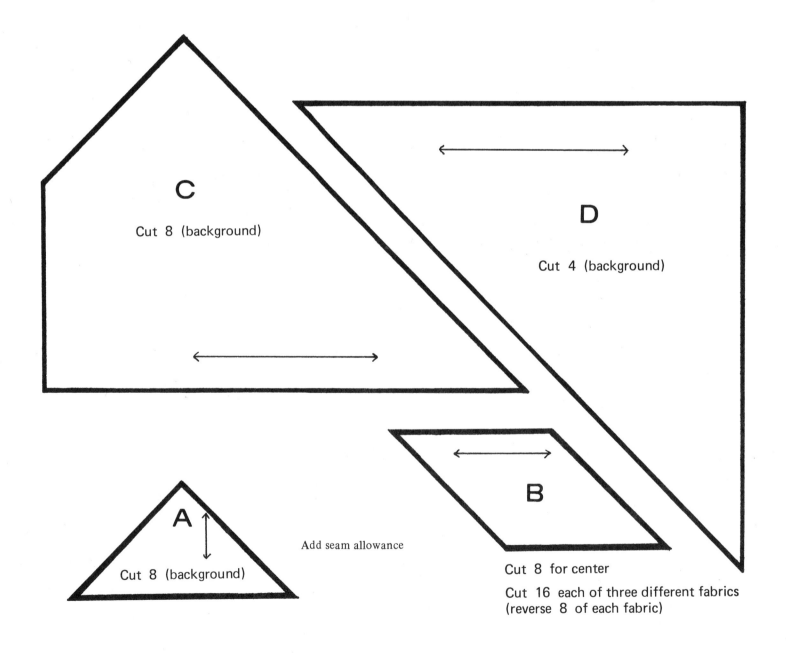

C

Cut 8 (background)

D

Cut 4 (background)

A

Cut 8 (background)

Add seam allowance

B

Cut 8 for center

Cut 16 each of three different fabrics
(reverse 8 of each fabric)

Curved Seam Work

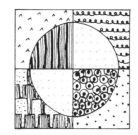

On the following pages are traditional patterns with curved seams. When handling curved seams, special techniques are necessary. In the discussion below, we've used Drunkard's Path to illustrate these techniques. They will be helpful when doing any patterns involving curved seams.

DRUNKARD'S PATH

DESIGN AND COLOR VARIATIONS

The basic pattern of a square with a circle set in one corner can produce dazzling patchwork. It is stunning when done in solid colors, or with one solid color and one print. Sometimes more than two fabrics can be used, and again the results are outstanding. It is almost a pattern with which you and your fabrics can't go wrong. Usually the blocks are assembled with light and dark fabrics alternating. Some authorities on patchwork stress using fabrics with sharp color contrasts. However, equally beautiful work can result from either combining a variety of prints or using an assortment of both soft and subtle colors. Feel free to experiment using the fabrics of your choice. Try to make up some of your own arrangements by assembling several blocks and then laying them out in various designs. The following pages show a few of the many results that can be obtained.

SUITABLE FABRICS

Closely woven cottons or cotton/polyesters will work up most easily, but if you are considering making a quilt or comforter from the 4 or 5 inch pattern, double knits are ideal. They can be machine assembled and, because of the knit construction, are easy to piece on the curve.

TEMPLATE MAKING, TRACING ONTO THE FABRIC

Choose from the three different pattern sizes given on pages 84 and 85. The larger size is a good choice for a quilt-size project.

Transfer the two pattern pieces onto the smooth side of a sheet of sandpaper. Cut the patterns out and set them aside. Repeat this process a second time and add a ¼ inch seam allowance to all the edges. Cut out this second set of patterns. Be sure that you have copied the notch on the curved edge of each pattern piece. When tracing the pattern onto your fabric, first trace around the pattern with the added-on seam allowance. The smaller pattern piece can then be centered inside the first drawn shape and traced around. Let your pencil fall into the cut-away notch. The outside pencil line will be your cutting line, while the remaining inside pencil line will serve as your stitching line.

ASSEMBLING

Pin the two fabric pieces together with three pins. Match the sewing lines at the center notches and at both sides where the pencil lines meet. Careful pinning at this point will enable you to easily stitch the two pieces together. Your finished block should make a perfect square. Be sure to use small stitches for your hand sewing. It is usually unnecessary to clip the convex curve. The circular seam will lie flat if the fabric isn't stiff or bulky. Sew the blocks together, stitching from fabric edge to fabric edge.

FINISHING

Items made from this pattern can be finished with either a bound or ruffled edge, or in any manner of your choice.

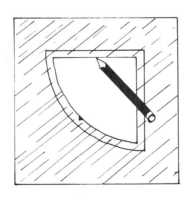
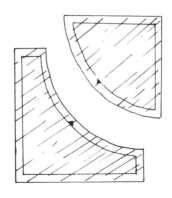
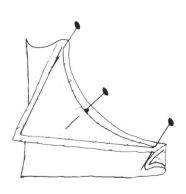

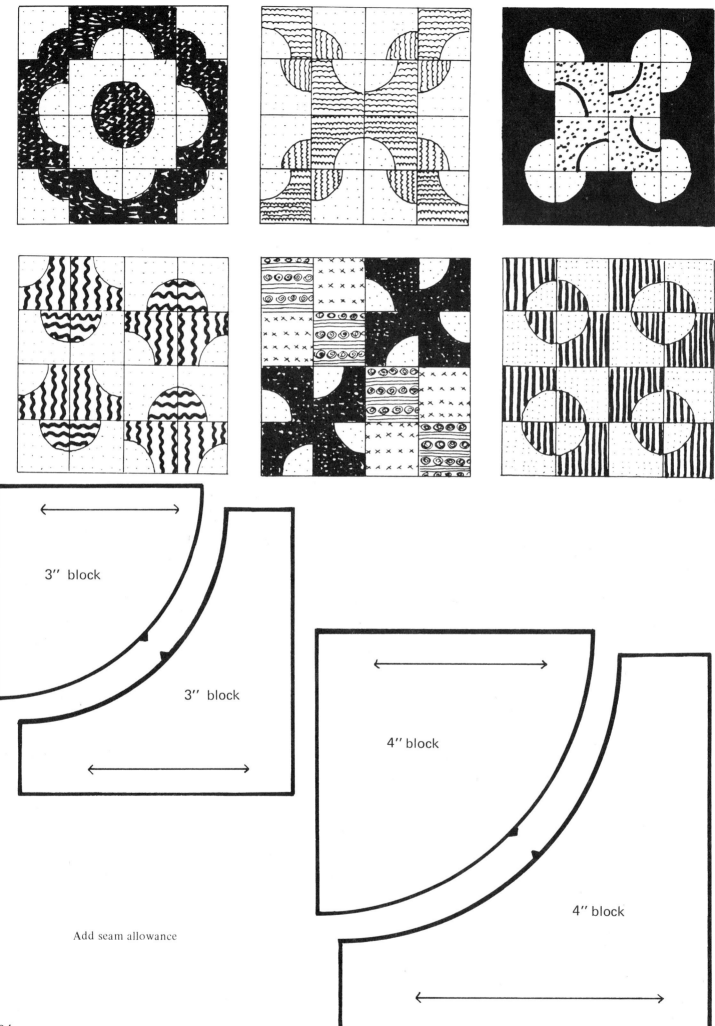

3" block

3" block

4" block

4" block

Add seam allowance

Drunkard's Path

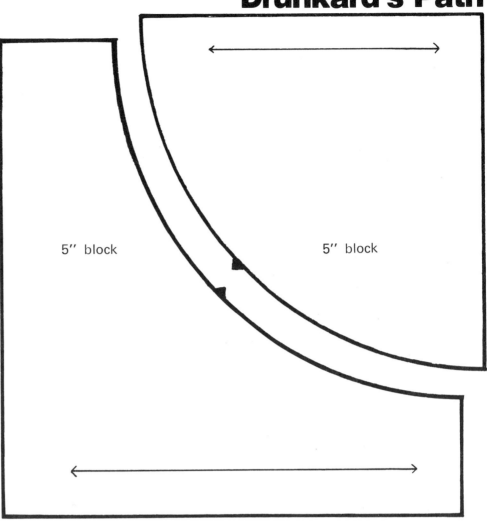

5″ block

5″ block

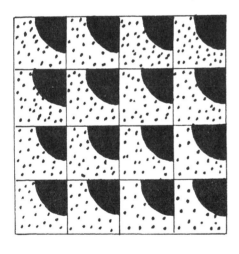
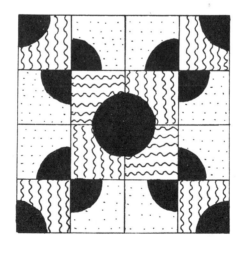
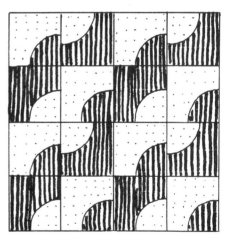

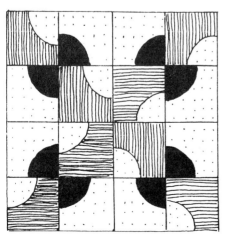
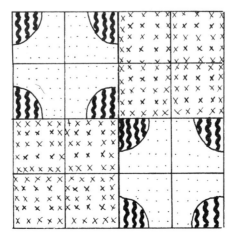
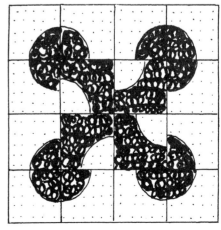

Jinx Star

12" square
See Color Plate on Page 73

Repeat of four blocks with bands

Repeat of four blocks

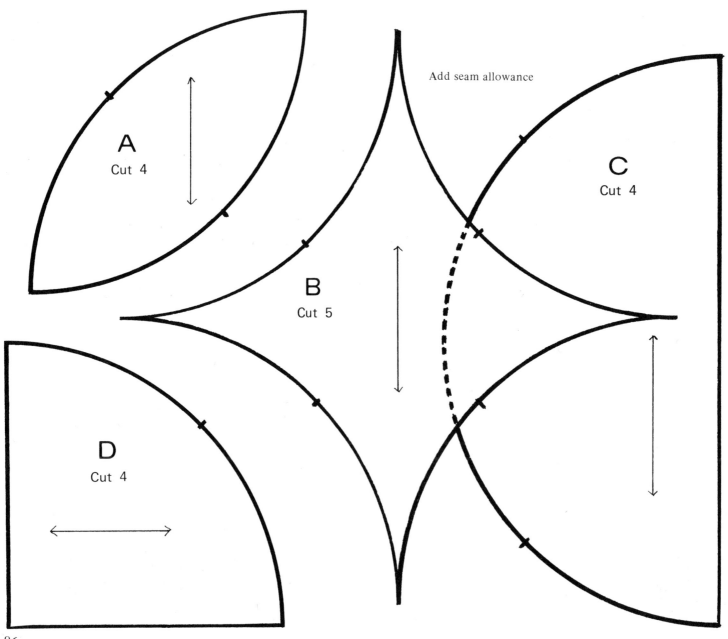

Add seam allowance

A
Cut 4

B
Cut 5

C
Cut 4

D
Cut 4

Robbing Peter To Pay Paul

Repeat of four blocks
See Color Plate on Page 73

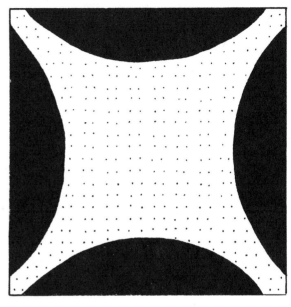

12" square

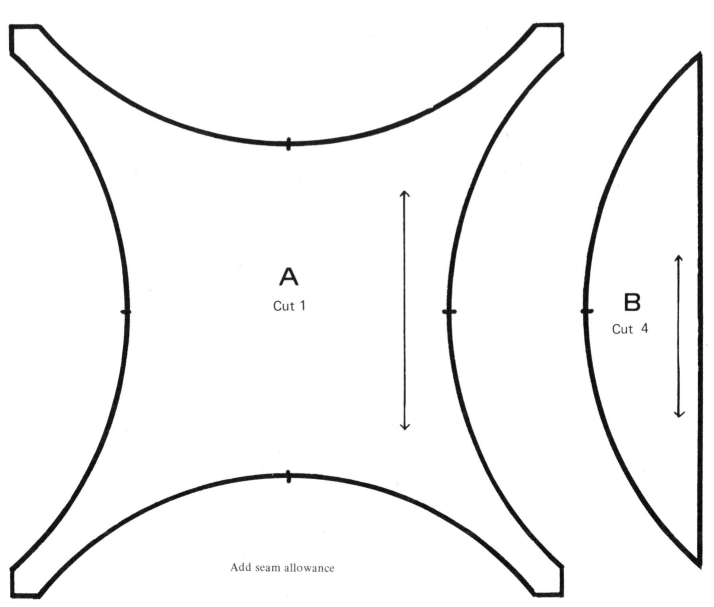

A
Cut 1

B
Cut 4

Add seam allowance

Spools

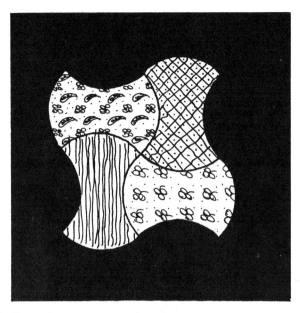

Four shapes pieced and appliqued
to a background fabric

See Color Plates on Pages 69 & 72

Yardage of continous shapes

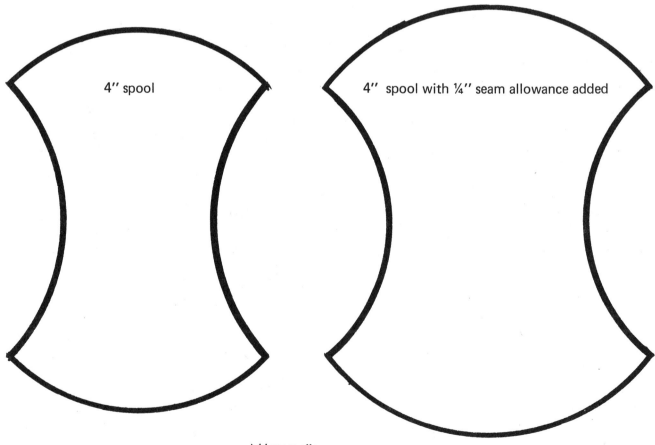

4'' spool

4'' spool with ¼'' seam allowance added

Add seam allowance

Glorified Nine Patch

14" square

Repeat of four units
See Color Plate on Page 73

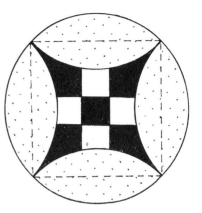

One unit (circle or squared off)

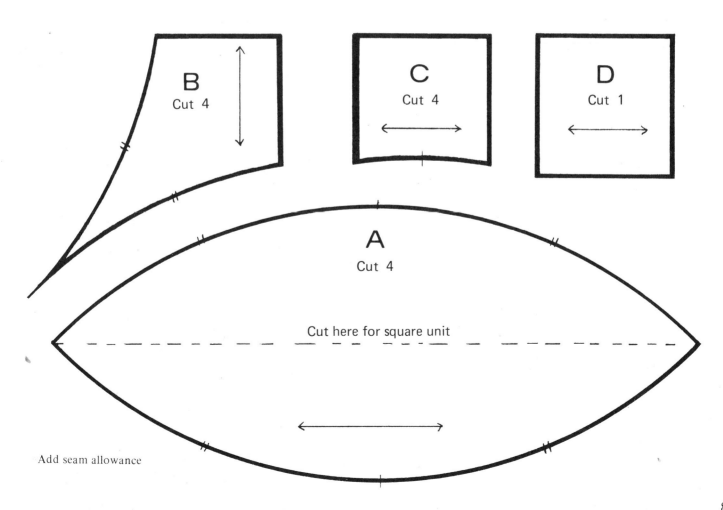

B
Cut 4

C
Cut 4

D
Cut 1

A
Cut 4

Cut here for square unit

Add seam allowance

Clamshell

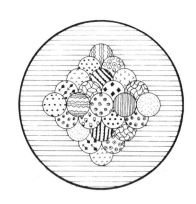

CONSIDER DESIGN AND COLOR VARIATIONS FOR YOUR PROJECT

We prefer to treat the clamshell as an applique rather than pieced work. Clamshells must always be placed in straight rows, somewhat resembling fish scales. If you are creative you won't be limited by the rows, as many arrangements can still be successfully carried out. Different suggested arrangements are shown here, and our students have created many other novel designs. Color plate 51 shows the clamshells arranged in diagonal rows. Besides being utilized in household items, clamshells can be used to trim or add accents to garments. Plate 68 illustrates a child's dress beautifully decorated with a yoke of delicate clamshells.

The more prints and fabrics you manage to work into your total design, the richer your end product will be. Fabrics with large printed areas, usually not suitable for most patchwork, will blend beautifully into the clamshell motif. We encourage students, especially those with limited funds or limited access to fabrics of certain colors, to study the back side or the "wrong side" of their fabrics. A sprinkling of "wrong sides" of prints, along with the right side of the same fabric, will stretch your dollar and increase your design potential. The sleeves and yoke of the caftan in plate 27 have a good mixture of right and wrong sides, yet the untrained eye would not realize this clever device. As you can see from the color photo, the wrong side of the printed fabric gives a finished appearance of softer coloring, hence a nice quaintness about the item. One student became so enrapt with her "wrong sides" that she designed her whole clamshell project with them.

Another trick you will quickly see the advantage of is adding fabrics with a cream or white background. This will give you access to more fabrics, which in turn will add richness to your end product. Plate 82 shows a clamshell pillow utilizing the blue and brown color families. Notice it has many patches with white or cream backgrounds with each containing only a small amount of brown or blue. The total effect is still very successful, so don't be afraid to experiment with fabrics you think are only borderline choices.

SUITABLE FABRICS

Fabrics for the clamshell pattern should be closely woven and light in weight. If a fabric is sheer, it will need to be underlined. If this is the case, the two fabrics would be handled as one. Try to find a variety of prints ranging from small overall patterns to spotty and even large prints. Review page 4 on selecting assorted prints.

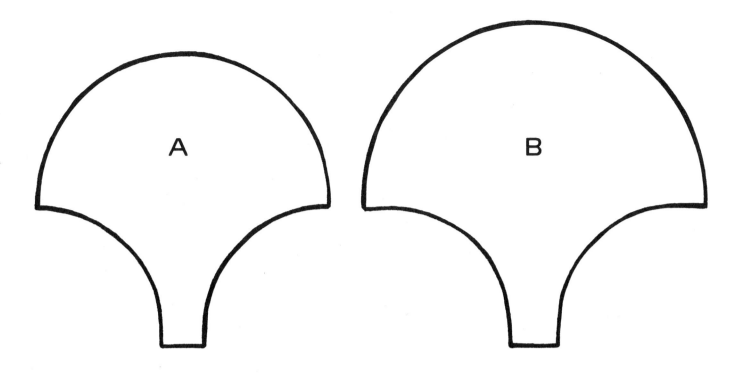

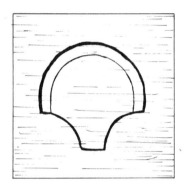

TEMPLATE MAKING, TRACING ONTO THE FABRIC

Two pattern pieces are needed. Pattern A above, is the actual finished clamshell size, while pattern B will give you a turn-under allowance along the top curved edge. Make a sturdy template of each size.

Trace around the larger pattern piece (B) on the right side of your fabric. This will be your cutting edge. Next set the smaller pattern in place and trace only around the top or curved edge. This will be your turn-under line. You will find that fabrics will be easier to handle if you <u>trace all the B's, then the A's and then cut them out.</u>

Finger press back the seam allowance to your turn-under line and baste in place. Try to baste the edge back so it forms a smooth, continuous curve. The edges of the two lower curves are not turned under but are left flat. When all of your clamshells are prepared in this manner you can start to design your layout.

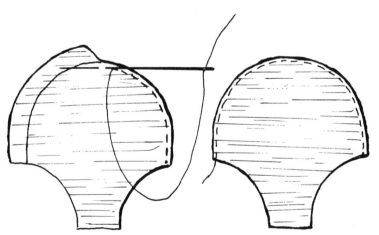

Front view — Basting back the seam allowance

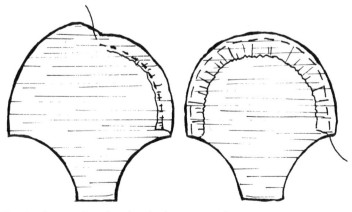

Back view — Basting back the seam allowance

PREPARE THE FOUNDATION ON WHICH TO APPLIQUE THE SHELLS

We mentioned before that the clamshell pattern is really appliqued in place and not pieced, so why not applique and quilt all at once. To do this, prepare a three-layered foundation consisting of a top fabric, sheet batting and a bottom layer of fabric.

TOP LAYER. If the top layer of fabric will be completely covered with clamshells, try using a lightweight gingham or a fabric with a stripe. Let the stripes run horizontally, or follow the horizontal lines in the gingham to guide you when placing the clamshells in straight, horizontal rows.

If you plan to let some of the top fabric show as part of the total design, use a top fabric appropriate in color and texture. You can give yourself easy guidelines, even with a solid colored fabric, by using one of two methods:

Method 1: Machine baste horizontal rows 1½ inches apart across the entire top fabric. The machine basting can be easily removed once the clamshells are sewn in place.

Method 2: Place long strips of masking tape across the top fabric running horizontally. The base of the clamshells can be lined up with the tape. When the shells are properly in place and pinned securely, peel the masking tape away.

MIDDLE LAYER. Under the top fabric you will need a layer of firmly-woven sheet batting. This will give your clamshell design the puffed or quilted dimension that adds so much richness to the finished item.

BOTTOM LAYER. Beneath the batting will be a third fabric or a backing. Muslin or a cotton/polyester woven fabric will do. If the backing will be seen as in a quilt or table mat, use a nice fabric with a print or color that will enhance the top design.

The top fabric should be the size you want your finished item to be plus a seam allowance. Generally cut the batting and backing 1 inch larger on all sides for small projects such as purses, pillow tops, pockets, mats, etc. Cut the batting and backing 6 to 8 inches larger on all sides for large projects such as wall hangings, coverlets or quilts.

For greater accuracy, as needed when you do any part of a garment or you are working with a precise commercial pattern, lightly pencil in the seam lines on the top fabric. This small step will save you valuable time later on and will add to the ease of laying out the clamshells so you don't waste a lot of them in the seam allowance.

Hold the three-layered foundation together by pinning them, then baste through all the thicknesses about 1 to 1½ inches in from the top fabric's outer edge. For a large project such as a coverlet or quilt baste them in the same manner as you would when preparing a quilt top, batting and backing for quilting.

PRACTICE YOUR LAYOUT DESIGN

Lay the clamshells out in rows starting with the top row and working from left to right. The top of each clamshell should be in a straight line and their sides should just be touching. The second row starts about 1½ inches below the first row. The center top edge of each shell in the second row should meet the touching sides of the row above.

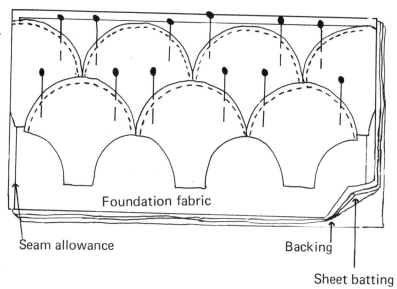

Foundation fabric

Seam allowance

Backing

Sheet batting

Arrange all the clamshells in this manner. If you need a better overall pattern, you can rearrange them or cut and prepare more as your design dictates. Once your practice layout is perfect, carefully remove the clamshells starting with the bottom row. Then remove the next row. A good way to keep the shells in their proper order is to stack them together using a clothespin or a large safety pin. When stacking the shells, start with the far left shell; place the one to its right under it, the next under the second and so on. Press a small piece of masking tape to the top of each stack of shells giving the stack a number such as no. 10, then no. 9, no. 8, etc.

FINISHING

Reposition rows 1 and 2, using two pins to keep each clamshell from twisting. Applique down row 1 with the running stitch shown below. Arrange row 3, pin, then applique row 2 in place. Continue in this manner until all the clamshells have been stitched.

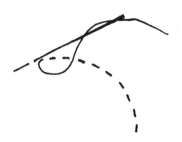

Plate 70. The same Mexican Star pattern was used in the above photos. The nine squares in the center stand out more when the colors are alternated as in the photo on the left. By Marjorie Puckett. The color placement in the handbag on the right creates an illusion of longer strips in the center going toward the corners. By Dorothy Denton.

Plate 71. Missouri Puzzle. By Joan Beucke.

Plate 72. Fish Circle. By Joan Beucke.

Plate 73. Christmas Star. By Marjorie Puckett.

Plate 74. Stars and Cubes. By Susan Bennett.

Gardener's Prize

16" block pieced and appliqued to a larger background

Repeat of four blocks

16" block with pieced background

See Color Plate on Page 97

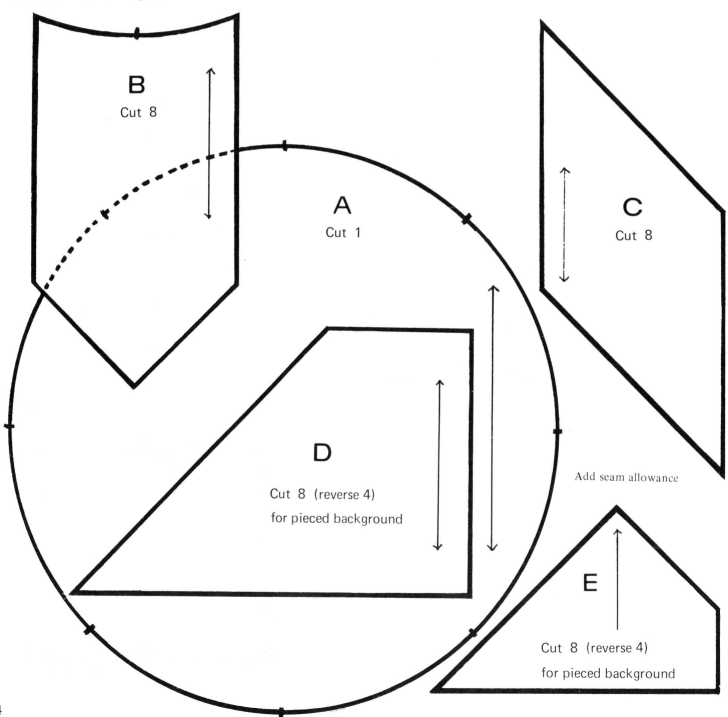

B
Cut 8

A
Cut 1

C
Cut 8

D
Cut 8 (reverse 4)
for pieced background

Add seam allowance

E
Cut 8 (reverse 4)
for pieced background

Star Flower

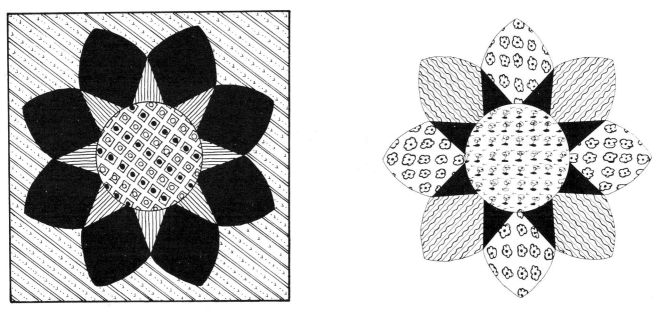

10'' design (good for applique)

See Color Plate on Page 96

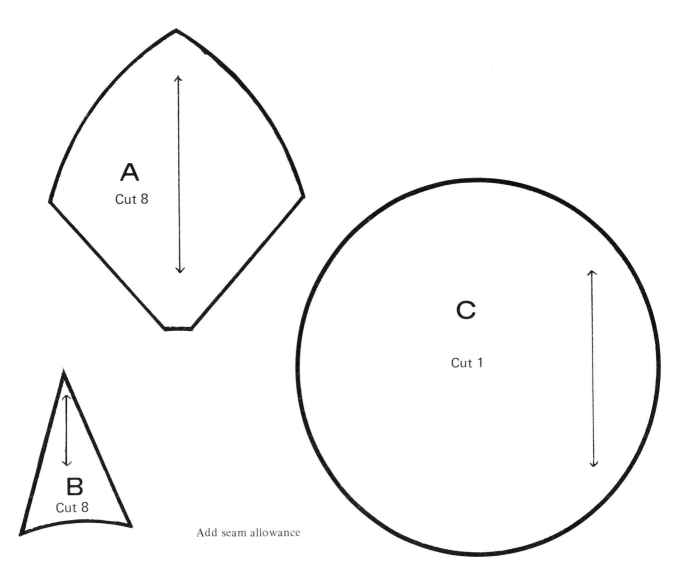

A
Cut 8

C
Cut 1

B
Cut 8

Add seam allowance

Plate 75. The handbag pattern was cut from yardage made from Clamshells. By Esther Spence.

Plate 76. Reds and browns highlight this 20-petal Dresden Plate mat. By Jessie Hoyt.

Plate 77. These four blocks of Cross and Crown show how a continuous pattern can emerge. By Donna Swenson.

Plate 78. This Squared Star in warm colors gives a lovely sunburst effect. By Marjorie Puckett.

Plate 79. Placemats, made with the 15-petal Dresden Plate pattern make a handsome table setting. By Pat Porter.

Plate 80. A random arrangement of Clamshells makes up the front for this toaster cover. By Janelle Kennedy.

Plate 81. The star flower is pieced and appliqued onto a background. In this example, the inside points were cut from the same background fabric. By Marjorie Puckett.

Plate 82. A clamshell pillow top bound in ultra suede. By Marjorie Puckett.

Plate 83. This 16-petal Dresden Plate was pieced and then appliqued onto yellow fabric to make this pillow top. By Patty Witte.

Plate 84. The Gardener's Prize pattern was pieced and then appliqued onto a background of ultra suede. By Marjorie Puckett.

Plate 85. Two variations of fabric placement make these two Lemon Star designs look quite different. Left by Odessa Hylton, right by Donna Swenson. A Rail Fence tablecloth is shown as a backdrop. By Phyllis Gustafsson and Gladys Schnirring.

Dresden Plate

Edge finished in scallops
Appliqued onto background

Edge finished in points
Good when lined, for placemats

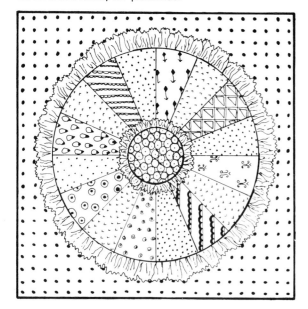

Edge finished in smooth circle
Ruffle trim added

See Color Plates on Pages 96, 97, & 100

Four petal sizes are given, each offering a choice of three edge finishes. A 2" or larger center is appliqued on top of the plate after the petals are joined.

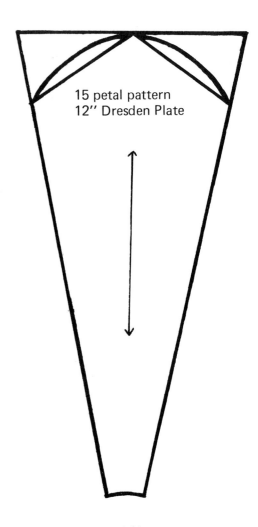

15 petal pattern
12" Dresden Plate

Add seam allowance

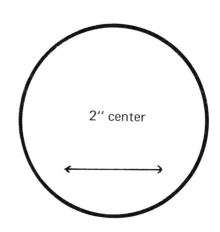

2" center

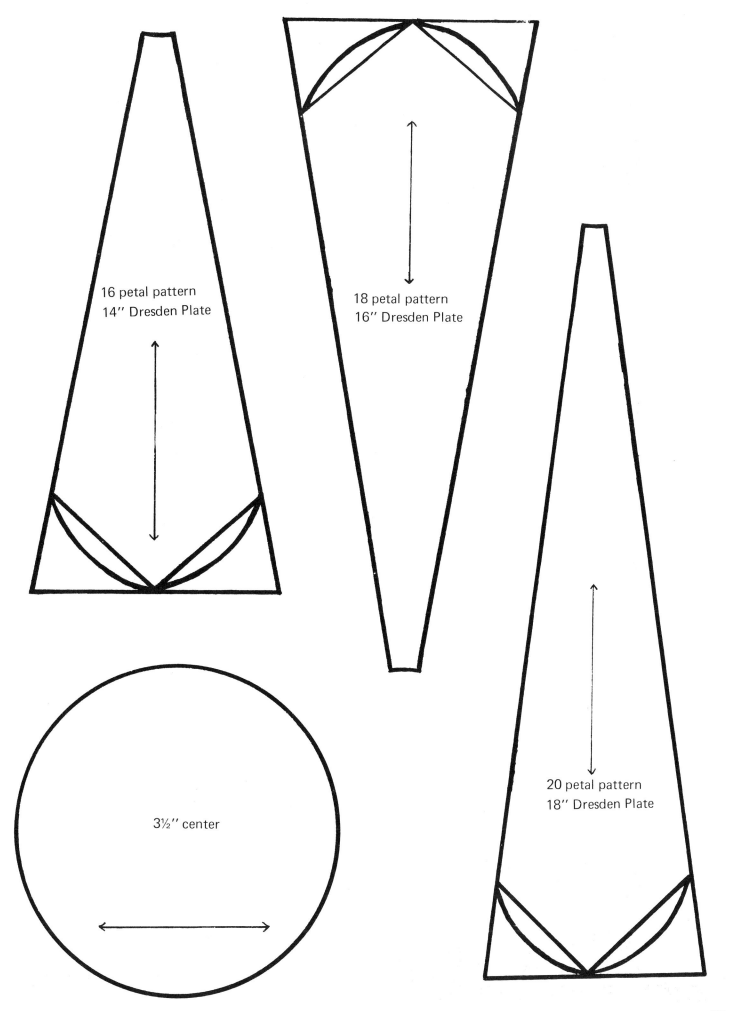

16 petal pattern
14″ Dresden Plate

18 petal pattern
16″ Dresden Plate

20 petal pattern
18″ Dresden Plate

3½″ center

Plate 86. Morning Star. By Lois Jensen.

Plate 87. The circular movement of the Clamshells blends nicely with this pillow shape. By Sue Staton.

Plate 88. A 16-petal Dresden Plate is appliqued onto a tote bag. By Cookie Lyou.

Plate 89. Edgings of lace add to the delicacy of this 16-petal Dresden Plate appliqued to a pillow top. By Judy Johnson.

Plate 90. Red and white patchwork pillows give interest to this girl's room. Patchwork by JoAnne Wolff, Phyllis Davis, and Sue Staton.

Plate 91. Pastel pillows using the basic triangle shape. Left by Odessa Hylton, right by Myrna Schatzman, and top by Betty Mitchell.